TAO

OF

ISLAM

Ali Hussain

Tao of Islam

ISBNs
Paperback 979-8-9986884-0-9
Hardback 979-8-9986884-1-6
Digital 979-8-9986884-2-3

Disclaimer: The contents of this book are shared with the sincerest intention to inspire, enlighten, and provoke thoughtful reflection. However, the ideas, practices, and insights presented here are not offered as prescriptions, directives, or absolute truths. They are the reflections and understandings of mine, drawn from personal experiences, spiritual explorations, and careful study.

I dedicate this book firstly to my Creator, the Supreme Being, the Exalted One, the Cosmic Essence of all, the divine Love and Mercy of all, the All-Omnipotent Force, to the One whom all is due, to the one and only Lord of the universe!

In loving memory of my two best buds.
Zain Hussain July 5th, 2009–April 11th, 2014
Salman Ali Sheraze January 21st, 1980–August, 14th, 2016

CONTENTS

Author's note

The teachings and practices described in this book are not a substitute for professional advice, whether medical, legal, financial, or spiritual. If you are considering any changes to your lifestyle, health, or practices based on the content of this book, I urge you to seek guidance from qualified professionals and conduct thorough research before proceeding.

PROLOGUE

"Me. We." –Muhammad Ali, Harvard University, 1975

Tao, also known as dao, is a Chinese term that can be translated to mean "the way," "the path," or "the principle." It has been central to Chinese philosophy and culture for thousands of years. In traditional Chinese thought, "tao" refers to the natural order or principle that underlies the universe and guides all things. It is often associated with the idea of living in harmony with nature and following the natural rhythms of life.

People often describe the concept of tao as something that is both transcendent and immanent, present in all things but also beyond any one thing. It's considered the ultimate reality that encompasses everything and yet cannot be fully understood or described in words. Tao has been the subject of much study and contemplation throughout Chinese history and has influenced many aspects of Chinese culture, including religion, philosophy, art, literature, and martial arts. In practical terms, "tao" can be used to describe the way or path that someone or something follows to achieve a particular goal. For example, in martial arts, "tao" might refer to the specific techniques and principles that a practitioner follows to achieve mastery. Bruce Lee's book, *Tao of Jeet Kun Do,* is his interpretation of the essence of his particular martial arts discipline.

Taoism has impacted the world by promoting principles of tranquility, balance, and living in alignment with awareness, shaping concepts of health, energy (Qi), and interconnectedness. Taoist ideas spread across Asia, influencing Zen Buddhism and many aspects of Japanese society and Korean traditions, and inspired global practices like mindfulness, minimalism, and ecological awareness. Its focus on simplicity and flow resonates worldwide, transcending cultural boundaries. Taoism influences promote compassion,

1

unity, and selfless service as natural expressions of living in harmony with the Tao.

Islam is a monotheistic religion founded by Prophet Muhammad (PBUH—Peace be Upon Him) in the Arabian Peninsula in the 7th century. Its followers, known as Muslims, believe in one singular creator with no equals and consider the Quran to be the holy book to which Muslims look to as a divine compass.

The central message of Islam emphasizes submission to the will of God, with the goal of a Muslim's life being to worship and submit to God. Muslims strive to live according to God's teachings and guidance, as revealed in the Quran, while also following the example set by Prophet Muhammad (PBUH). They believe that this life serves as a test and that their ultimate aim is to please God and attain Paradise in the Hereafter. The Five Pillars of Islam form the foundation of the Muslim faith and practice. These five pillars are as follows:

1. Shahada - the declaration of faith
2. Salat - prayer
3. Sawm - fasting during the month of Ramadan
4. Zakat - giving to charity
5. Hajj - pilgrimage to Mecca at least once in a lifetime for those who are able

The Five Pillars of Islam focus on moral and ethical conduct, which includes respect for parents and elders, honesty, justice, and charity. Muslims are encouraged to lead a balanced life that encompasses worship, family, work, compassion, kindness, community, and social responsibility toward all of God's creation. Islam is currently the second-largest religion in the world, with over two billion followers, and it is also the fastest-growing religion globally. Muslims come from diverse backgrounds and cultures, with Islam boasting a rich history and traditions that has influenced art, literature, science, and philosophy.

Embracing Islam has brought me transformative healing, an unmatched sense of beauty, and serenity. The practice of daily prayers, mindful rituals, and the constant remembrance of Allah have woven a sense of peace into the fabric of my life. The teachings of Islam offer not only spiritual guidance but also a holistic approach to well-being, cultivating a harmonious balance between body, mind, and soul. In sharing my journey, I aim to convey the enlightening power of Islam, which has illuminated my path with purpose and inner tranquility, guiding me toward a life rooted in compassion, discipline, and unwavering faith. I will also provide a thoughtful comparative analysis of Islam alongside some of the world's major religions. Through this exploration, I seek to expand the often limited and sometimes misunderstood perceptions of Islam, not only among non-Muslims but also within the diverse Muslim community itself, including both practicing and non-practicing individuals. By highlighting the common threads and distinct values that Islam shares with other faiths, I hope to cultivate a deeper understanding and appreciation of its philosophical teachings. This analysis will serve as a bridge, connecting the shared spiritual aspirations of humanity while illuminating the unique contributions of Islam to the global religious landscape. In doing so, I aspire to challenge misconceptions and encourage a more informed, nuanced, and respectful dialogue about the faith.

I would like to discuss what I believe to be the essence and the correlation between traditional Islam and the *Tao of Islam*. Islam is a religion that includes peace, tolerance, respect, and mercy. I will provide a non-dualistic perspective and philosophy that recognizes the fundamental unity or non-separation of theology.

The focus of this literature will emphasize the interconnectedness and interdependencies, transcending the conventional distinctions and dualities that arise from our conceptual thinking. I believe that ultimate reality or truth cannot be fully captured or understood through binary concepts and that there is a deeper underlying unity that encompasses all apparent differences. My motive is to reveal the holistic, mental, physical, metaphysical, and spiritual benefits associated with the practices and principles of Islam. Let the *Tao of Islam* be a beacon, not just for Muslims, but for all who seek a life of harmony, where the Tao and Islam converge in discipline, balance, and moral excellence.

If my words do not bring you closer to Islam, may they bring you closer to God—and if not to God, then at least to yourself, to that quiet within you that still believes in something sacred. I do not write to convert you but to invite you—not to replace your path but to help you walk it with more light. If nothing else, pray I can help you be a better Christian, Jew, or even just a better person

If you are Muslim, may your prayer feel alive again. If you are Christian, may Christ's love burn clearer in your heart. If you are Jewish, may the covenant rise strong in your blood. And if you are Buddhist, Hindu, Taoist, or Sikh, may you recognize the One light behind all names. Even if you carry doubt or call yourself nothing at all—may you remember that even silence has a center, and even doubt has direction.

Throughout history, seekers of truth have recognized an underlying order within existence—a sacred rhythm that governs the cosmos and all that lies within it. Islam and Taoism, though distinct in their expressions, both point toward a fundamental truth: surrendering to the divine flow brings harmony, purpose, and peace.

In the grand design of existence, the truest wisdom is not in forcing life to conform to our will but in aligning our will with the divine flow—the essence of both Islamic qadr and Taoist wisdom.

"The more you know, the more you realize you don't know." –Aristotle

4

INTRODUCTION

"When you are favored by God, you're also favored by the devil...you just got to be strong and stay on the right side..."

– Mike Tyson

DISCOVERING THE TAO OF ISLAM

"Do not go where the path may lead, go instead where there is no path and leave a trail." –Emerson

To walk the Tao of Islam is to surrender to the flow behind all things. It is to recognize that life does not unravel by chance or chaos but by a sacred current, divine in origin and perfect in design. In Islam, this concept is known as qadr "QAH-dur," or divine decree—the understanding that everything in existence unfolds according to God's infinite wisdom and will. In Taoism, a similar idea is found in the concept of Tao (The Way)—the natural flow of the universe that one must align with rather than resist. Both traditions emphasize that true peace is not found in controlling life but in submitting to its higher order. In the Quran, Allah declares: "Indeed, We have created everything according to a determined measure." (Quran 54:49)

Qadr is the recognition that every event, every breath, and every moment has been divinely ordained. This does not negate free will; rather, it acknowledges that human effort exists within a larger divine framework. A person may make choices, but the ultimate unfolding of events is guided by Allah's wisdom. The essence of faith in Islam is to trust this decree—knowing that even hardship carries purpose and ease will follow.

When one accepts qadr, they release unnecessary resistance to life. Anxiety and fear lessen, for the believer knows that nothing happens except by Allah's will and that each experience, whether joyous or painful, is an opportunity for spiritual growth. This sentiment is echoed thoughtfully by the words of Joe Rogan when speaking of Muslims "They're so devout in their religious beliefs, they have so much confidence. It's almost like that's all taken care of; they can just concentrate on what they do. God has a plan for everything; you don't have to have this existential angst that a lot of people roll around through life with."

Similarly, in Taoism, Tao represents the ultimate source and principle of all existence—the natural, unforced unfolding of life. The Tao Te Ching, the foundational text of Taoism, states:

"Those who flow as life flows know they need no other force." (Laozi)

Taoism teaches that struggling against life—trying to force what is not meant to be—creates suffering. Instead, true wisdom is found in Wu Wei (effortless action)—aligning with the Tao rather than resisting it. This does not mean passivity but rather a deep awareness of when to act and when to allow things to unfold naturally. When a river meets an obstacle, it does not fight against it but flows around it, continuing its course. A person aligned with the Tao moves through life in the same way—adapting, trusting, and flowing without unnecessary struggle.

Though qadr and Tao emerge from different religious frameworks, they point toward the same truth:

- There is a divine order in life.
- Peace comes from trusting and surrendering to that order.
- Struggle against reality leads to suffering while flowing with it leads to contentment.

Islam encourages believers to have tawakkul "ta-WUK-kool" (trust in Allah)—a concept deeply parallel to Taoism's Wu Wei. Just as the Taoist seeks to align with the natural flow of life, the Muslim seeks to align their will with Allah's decree, knowing that His wisdom surpasses human understanding.

Surrendering Without Losing Agency

While both traditions advocate trust and surrender, neither promotes fatalism. In Islam, the Prophet Muhammad (PBUH) said: "Tie your camel and trust in Allah." (Tirmidhi 2517)

This teaches that faith is not about abandoning effort but about recognizing that after all due effort is made, the outcome rests in divine hands. In Taoism, this is akin to knowing when to act decisively and when to let go, understanding that not all things are meant to be controlled.

Both qadr and Tao provide a spiritual approach to navigating life's uncertainties. Whether facing hardship, making decisions, or pursuing goals, the key lies in trusting the process—working diligently while accepting what unfolds. The art of surrender does not mean giving up; rather, it means understanding where human effort ends and divine orchestration begins.

This journey is one of discovery, introspection, and transformation, and I invite you to join me in exploring this rich tradition—not as an authoritative guide but as a deeply personal reflection on faith and spirituality.

Having spent a significant part of my life observing diverse cultures, traditions, and religions across the world, I have been blessed with the opportunity to immerse myself in various spiritual practices. My journey has led me to experience the richness of different faiths—fasting, praying, and seeking truth in Buddhist monasteries, Christian churches, Jewish synagogues, and Hindu temples. These diverse encounters have deepened my understanding of the spiritual truths that flow through all religions.

Much like the heavyweight boxing champion Muhammad Ali so eloquently expressed: "Rivers, lakes, ponds, streams, and oceans all have different names, but they all contain water. So do religions have different names, and they all contain truth expressed in different ways, forms, and at different times. It doesn't matter whether you're a Muslim, a Christian, or a Jew; when you believe in God, you should believe that all people are part of one family." Ali's profound sentiment reflects a core belief that resonates deeply within me: *that all religions, though expressed through different traditions and languages, contain a shared truth and are paths leading toward the same divine essence.*

The principle of this belief can be distilled from (Quran 5:48) "For every community We have appointed a [divine] law and a way. Had Allah willed, He would have made you one community [united in religion], but [He intended] to test you in what He has given you; so race to [all that is] good. To Allah is your return all together, and He will [then] inform you concerning that over which you used to differ."

I humbly acknowledge that I am neither a scholar nor a theologian, nor do I claim to be highly educated or extensively well-read. I approach this work not as an authority on Islam, Taoism, or any specific group but simply as an individual seeking to share my personal reflections. The thoughts, interpretations, and perceptions expressed within these pages are entirely my own, and I make no claim to represent the official stance of Islam or any particular community.

I recognize that, like everyone, I am flawed, and, at times, my actions may not fully align with the ideals I strive to embody. There may even be instances where I appear hypocritical. Yet, my intentions are grounded in sincerity and love, aiming to encourage open discourse and dialogue. My hope is to share my understanding of Islam with humility in the spirit of building bridges and deepening mutual respect.

In sharing this reflection, I seek to illuminate the numinous core of Islam—a faith that harmonizes the mind, body, and soul. My purpose is not to present an authoritative stance but rather to offer my perspective with the hope that it may resonate with others who are on their own spiritual journeys. I believe wholeheartedly in a loving, compassionate, and merciful Creator whose essence transcends the limitations of human understanding. To me, the essence of faith lies in living a life grounded in courage, service, compassion, and love—universal values that echo through every religion.

I wish to articulate the depth and breadth of Islam, the way of Islam, or, as I like to say, the *Tao of Islam* from my perspective. I hope to shine a light on some of the beauty within Islamic principles, practices, and rituals that seem to have become obscure. Also, to diminish stigmas and clarify many misconceptions that may be associated with Islam. One common misconception, contrary to common belief, is that *Allah* is the name of God in Islam. The reality is that *Allah* is a word that means God in the Arabic language, which is a Semitic language, just as Aramaic and Hebrew are. The term *Allah* is not specific to Islam. Today, Arabic speakers from all religious backgrounds—Jews, Christians, and Muslims alike—all use the word *Allah* to mean God. However, Muslims do ascribe that Allah is solely unique to the one true God. Also, coincidentally, the word for God in Aramaic is *Alaha*. In Hebrew, *Eloah* is the word that means God.

Allah, Alaha, and Eloah sound similar when spoken. They share similar phonetic elements and sounds. Ironically, Jesus most likely referred to God as Alaha, as Aramaic was his native tongue. Arabic Christians to this day use the term *Allah* in their prayers, Bibles, and churches, showing its continuity as a term for God among Semitic-speaking peoples. Throughout this literature, I will use the words *God* and *Allah* interchangeably.

I do not attempt to define the Creator by name, for I believe the divine is beyond the grasp of human comprehension. Yet, I trust wholeheartedly in the benevolence of the Creator, who, in my conviction, embraces and accepts all those who live a life of goodness, love, and service—regardless of the specific name by which they address the divine or the particular doctrine they follow. It is my deep belief that God does not turn away from those who strive for righteousness and service to others, even if their expression of faith differs. Ultimately, love, compassion, and service form the essence of our connection to the divine, no matter the religious path we walk.

"The Tao that can be told is not the eternal Tao. The name that can be named is not the eternal name." (Tao Te Ching 1)

Jews accept Abraham, Isaac, and Jacob, among others, as prophets and Moses as a central prophet who brought forth the Torah. Jews do not accept Jesus as a messiah or a prophet, nor does he hold significance in Judaism. Christians accept Abraham, Isaac, and Jacob, among others, as prophets and

Moses as a central prophet who brought forth the Torah and Jesus as the Messiah and the Son of God and, in many cases, God himself. Muslims accept Abraham, Isaac, and Jacob, among others, as prophets and Moses as a central prophet who brought forth the Torah. Muslims also believe that Jesus is a prophet of God and that he taught what was revealed in the Old Testament. Muslims also believe Muhammad (PBUH) was a prophet who came after Jesus to continue and complete his teachings

Islam, Judaism, and Christianity are three Abrahamic religions that share a common origin, intertwined history, and theological underpinning. All three believe in one God, have sacred scriptures, and emphasize prayer, charity, and virtuous actions. Islam and Judaism consider themselves closely related due to a common ancestor, Abraham, and share historical and theological beliefs such as prophethood and the Day of Judgment. Mainstream Christianity views Jesus Christ as the Son of God and the savior, setting it apart from the other two. Despite differences, they share similarities, like monotheism, moral codes, and belief in an afterlife. However, there are also a significant number of Christians who do not believe that Jesus is God but rather a messenger of God.

There are those within the Jewish tradition who recognize Islam not as a new or foreign religion but as a continuation of ancient truth. In Jewish theology, there exists a concept known as B'nei Noach—the Children of Noah—those who, though not Jewish, live in accordance with the universal divine law given to humanity through the Prophet Noah long before Sinai.

The core of this path includes reverence for One God, justice, mercy, and moral restraint. Many rabbis, including the revered Maimonides (Rambam), acknowledged that Islam—through its absolute monotheism, ethical law, and deep reverence for prophets—fulfills and upholds this ancient covenant.

In this light, Islam is not simply a new revelation but a resurfacing of primordial submission. It is a return to that original current—a surrender that began not with the birth of religion but with the first breath of a soul that knew its Source. The Quran calls this Islam, meaning surrender, and the Taoists call it the Tao—the Way.

Whether through Noah, Abraham, Jesus, or Muhammad, the river is the same. What changes is the name we give the wind that carries us back to God.

In the rich and intricate tapestry of human spirituality, Islam emerges as a vibrant, vital thread, interweaving elements of discipline, devotion, and revelatory depth. Across the earth, countless Muslims hold their faith in high regard, cherishing the spiritual and moral framework it provides. Yet, despite the deep reverence many have for Islam, not everyone fully grasps or taps into the transformative beauty and power that it holds. Sadly, in some cases, the faith is viewed through a limited or dogmatic lens, obscuring the essence of its esoteric beauty, wisdom, and potential for personal growth.

As we navigate our modern era, where technology has brought the world closer and material comforts have become more easily accessible, a growing number of people are searching for deeper meaning. This yearning for inner peace, fulfillment, and spiritual enlightenment has become a defining feature of our time. It is no surprise that many seekers turn to Eastern philosophies like Taoism, Buddhism, and Hinduism, drawn to practices such as yoga and meditation for the sense of serenity and balance they provide. Yet, within Islam itself lies a treasure trove of spiritual practices that offer the same—if not deeper—pathways toward inner contemplation, well-being, and enlightenment.

Despite being the world's second-largest religion, Islam stands out not only for its rapid growth but also for having a high conversion rate among all faiths. Its structured discipline provides followers with a clear path, harnessing a deep sense of purpose and self-worth. Many individuals—ordinary and notable alike—are drawn to Islam's well-defined principles and practices, particularly those accustomed to rigorous discipline in their personal or professional lives. Its teachings, offering both spiritual depth and practical guidance, serve as a source of solace and enlightenment.

The impact of Islam's disciplined structure extends beyond personal spirituality. As Joe Rogan articulately expressed while on a podcast with Belal Muhammad, "Having a rigid schedule like that and having extreme discipline and having a real purpose, like when you are doing this to pray to God, and you have these five prayers you do during the day, it keeps you on the path. There's something to whatever Khabib is doing that's not just technique; it's not just that they are tough guys; there's also this devout sort of ideology that they have ascribed to that they live their life by."

This disciplined approach, deeply rooted in faith, resonates with a broad spectrum of people. In another podcast with Sean Strickland, Joe Rogan reiterated his respect for Islam's influence: "It's also that belief system that helps people, keeps them disciplined, keeps them on a good path. How many great fighters are devout Muslims...it's a pretty high percentage. It's a religion that embraces discipline 100 percent. You go through Ramadan and you're not eating all day, you're not drinking any water all day."

As the world witnesses a growing curiosity about Islam, it becomes clear that its teachings transcend boundaries. They appeal not just to those searching for faith but also to those striving for clarity, discipline, and purpose in an increasingly fast-paced world. The disciplined devotion that Rogan observes in Muslim fighters reflects a universal truth: a life lived with structure and a higher purpose is one that fosters strength, confidence, and inner peace. Islam, with its ascetic approach and practical guidance, continues to inspire millions to walk the path of resilience and faith.

In today's era of self-exploration and spiritual pursuit, practices like yoga, meditation, introspection, self-improvement, and holistic well-being have also found resonance within the Muslim community. These practices align with Islam's focus on inner reflection and growth. However, it is crucial that amidst this global spiritual awakening, we do not overlook the intricate richness and depth inherent in Islam itself. Beyond its rituals, Islam offers a comprehensive way of life centered around discipline, service to others, and gratitude.

Islam shares much common ground with other cultural and religious traditions, offering timeless wisdom and guidance. For those on a journey of self-discovery and seeking deeper meaning, Islam provides not just a set of rituals but a comprehensive framework for living a balanced and purposeful life. It serves as a source of truth and enlightenment for anyone in search of spiritual growth and fulfillment.

One of the most powerful aspects of Islam is the set of five binding pillars that form its foundation. These pillars are more than just rituals; they are a way of life. They guide Muslims in their relationship with God and with the world around them. In this work, I will take you through these five pillars, unpacking their significance and relevance in today's world. I will also present statistical, factual, and scientifically measurable data that supports and highlights the tangible benefits of practicing Islam—whether in terms of personal well-being, mental health, or the promotion of social harmony.

It is essential to remember that each individual's path is unique. What resonates with one person may not resonate with another. Therefore, I encourage every reader to approach this material with an open mind and a discerning heart. Investigate, reflect, and, most importantly, align your actions with your own inner wisdom and the knowledge you seek from trusted sources.

As seekers of truth, we are reminded that the journey of discovery requires humility, patience, and inquiry. May this book serve as a guidepost rather than a destination, illuminating possibilities while leaving you free to walk your path with intention and clarity.

Ultimately, trust in your Creator, your instincts, and the wisdom that unfolds when you seek knowledge with sincerity. The truth you uncover will be uniquely yours, shaped by your journey and your connection to the divine.

PEACE BE UPON YOU AND THE MERCY OF GOD AND HIS BLESSINGS

"When you are greeted with a greeting, greet in return with one better than it or [at least] return it [in a like manner]." (Quran 4:86)

Greetings and farewells are to be taken seriously in Islam; it is a religious obligation to greet one another and respond in kind. "Salaam alaikum," pronounced *sah-lahm ah-lay-koom*, is far more than just an ordinary greeting within the Islamic tradition. Meaning "peace be upon you," this Arabic expression conveys a deep, timeless sentiment of respect, goodwill, and the profound wish for peace to embrace the person being greeted. Rooted in the very heart of Islam, salaam alaikum goes beyond mere words—it is a spiritual gesture that signifies purity, safety, and an absence of harm or discord. The phrase "alaikum," meaning "upon you," carries with it the notion that the peace being extended is not a fleeting or casual wish but a shared, intentional offering—a universal desire for peace to envelop the recipient.

This highlights the interconnection between people, reaffirming the responsibility each individual carries in upholding peace and harmony within their community. In exchanging this greeting, Muslims engage in more than polite niceties; they affirm their commitment to embodying the values of tranquility, compassion, and goodwill. Salaam alaikum echoes the higher Islamic principles of mutual respect and kindness, gently reminding both the speaker and the recipient of the importance of cultivating peaceful relationships in every aspect of life—from personal interactions to the broader social fabric.

When we consider the meaning of peace in this context, it encompasses more than just an absence of conflict. It speaks to freedom from inner disturbances, the presence of mental calm, serenity, and release from oppressive or troubling thoughts. This harmonious concept of peace resonates on a spiritual and emotional level, making salaam alaikum a beautiful and sacred expression of sincere well-being.

This greeting is simple in its form but rich in its essence, embodying a sentiment of peace upon one's entire being. It is a refined, evolved, and eloquent vibration that aims to resonate deeply within a person's soul, imparting a genuine sentiment of care and well-being. In an ever-evolving world, this kind of greeting—whether expressed in Arabic or translated into English or any other language—carries powerful potential. To wish someone "peace be upon you" is more than a positive act; it is a conscious effort to uplift and center the soul, to speak a blessing into existence, and to have a sense of connection that transcends the ordinary. By embracing and sharing this sentiment, we contribute to a more harmonious world—one interaction at a time.

The customary response to the greeting "salaam alaikum" is "wa alaikum salaam," meaning "and upon you be peace." This reciprocal exchange not only reflects mutual respect but also reinforces the desire for peace, goodwill, and harmony between the individuals. In this response, there is an acknowledgment of the shared commitment to peace, where both the greeter and the recipient align themselves with the values of respect and tranquility, embodying the essence of Islamic teachings in human interaction.

What's particularly profound about this exchange is that it transcends mere words, evoking a deeper spiritual connection. By returning the greeting with "wa alaikum salaam," both parties implicitly recognize the presence of God in their interaction, affirming their shared understanding of divine peace and the sanctity of human relationships. This dialogue of peace is not just an external expression but also an invocation for inner calm and protection from harm for both the speaker and the listener.

Salaam alaikum is versatile in its usage. It is not only a greeting but can also be used as a farewell, making it applicable in both formal and informal contexts. Whether one is meeting someone for the first time or bidding them goodbye, the greeting encapsulates the desire for peace in every stage of human interaction. Moreover, it reflects a state of mindfulness, where believers are encouraged to extend peace and well-being to others at all times, promoting an atmosphere of compassion and unity.

Additionally, phrases such as "Allah-fiz," and "Huda-hafiz," meaning "may God be with you," are often used as alternatives. These phrases invoke divine protection and blessings upon the person being addressed, further cementing the presence of God's guidance in daily conversations. However, in modern times, the full beauty and intention of these greetings have sometimes been diminished, with many reducing "salaam alaikum" to simply "salaam," which translates as "peace." While this shortened version is still respectful, it does not fully encapsulate the rich layers of meaning, spirituality, and sincerity that the original greeting holds. Even salaam alaikum is a shortened version of "As-salaam alaikum wa Rahmatullahi wa Barakatuh," which translates to "Peace be upon you and the mercy and blessing of God."

In an age of hurried conversations, pausing to greet each other with the full weight of this blessing can elevate human interactions to something sacred, serving as a reminder of the greater purpose behind our words and actions. It's a sentiment that transcends language and culture—wherever we are, the act of wishing peace upon another being remains a powerful, timeless expression of love and goodwill.

Similarly, it's worth highlighting that "shlama" (pronounced *sh-la-ma*) is the Aramaic word for peace and is traditionally used as a greeting. Additionally, "shalom" (pronounced *sha-lom*) is the Hebrew term for peace, and it is often paired with "aleichem" to form the phrase "shalom aleichem," which directly translates to "peace be upon you." What is fascinating is that all three—shlama, shalom, and the Arabic salaam alaikum—share a common linguistic and cultural root, coming from the Semitic language family. The core concept expressed by these greetings is the same: peace, well-being, safety, and harmony.

Despite the slight variations in pronunciation, the essence of the greetings in Arabic, Aramaic, and Hebrew transcends linguistic boundaries. It is an expression of goodwill, a prayer for the recipient's peace of mind and soul. This alignment in language, culture, and sentiment serves as a subtle yet powerful reminder that peace is a universal aspiration deeply embedded in the fabric of these intertwined cultures.

What amazes me is how this commonality rarely gets the attention it deserves, especially when mainstream narratives often focus on the divisions—whether they be race, borders, or beliefs—that have arisen over time. The simplicity of these greetings, used by people from different faiths and cultures in the same region, reflects centuries of shared history and exchanges. And more importantly, it underscores the inherent desire for peace, respect, and unity across religious and ethnic divides.

In a world where differences are often emphasized, this linguistic and cultural connection poignantly reminds us of our shared humanity. At its core, it speaks to the deep-seated hope for a harmonious existence, showing us that, beyond our perceived differences, we are united by fundamental values of compassion and peace.

With an increasing number of scientists studying the nature of vibrations, frequencies, and the deeper workings of the quantum realm, we are rapidly coming to understand the immense power that our words and the vibrations they carry hold. Every sound, every spoken word, creates an energy that not only leaves a lasting impression on the listener but also reverberates within the speaker, influencing their physical and emotional state. Research shows that positive communication is not just beneficial for interpersonal relationships, but also for the health and well-being of the person speaking (Pitts & Socha, 2013). Many scientists now propose that everything in existence, from the smallest atom to the vast cosmos, is made up of energy, and this energy vibrates at different frequencies. The Law of Vibration postulates that all things, whether visible or invisible, tangible or ethereal, consist of pure energy or light, existing as distinct vibrational frequencies or patterns.

Notably, scientists have also found that these vibrations, and the electromagnetic energy associated with them, can induce changes within our cells, which can affect our overall bodily functions and well-being. For instance, researchers have identified how vibrations at a microscopic level, such as those in microtubules, can influence cellular morphology and, by extension, how our cells operate (Kučera O, Havelka D. "Mechano-electrical vibrations of microtubules—link to subcellular morphology." Biosystems. 2012). Microtubules are cellular highways, guiding movement, division, and neural activity—some theories even link them to consciousness. Such insights emphasize that the frequencies we interact with, even through something as simple as our speech, hold the potential to affect our very biology.

Considering these discoveries, it becomes evident that humanity should strive to elevate the vibrations within our words, thoughts, and actions. By raising our energetic frequency, especially through mindful communication, we have the power to uplift not only ourselves but also the communities we interact with, resonating on the highest possible plane of existence within this shared realm.

In this light, a greeting is not just a social formality—it is a potent tool for cultivating a more empathetic, compassionate, and harmonious society. It reminds us of our shared humanity and our duty to treat each other with dignity, kindness, and respect. By raising the energy and intention behind how we greet and interact with one another, we can elevate the collective vibration of our communities, developing a world where empathy, understanding, and connection flourish.

MAINSTREAM MANIPULATION

"The ability to see blinds us the most." –Ah Lee

Before delving into this next topic, I want to clarify that I do not intend to slander or criticize any religion, belief system, or community. Instead, I aim to shed light on how external forces such as media, politics, and economic agendas can distort and manipulate our perception of Islam or any religion for that matter. It is crucial to acknowledge that Islam, like all other faiths, has a complex history. There are episodes of violence associated with it, and yes, some Muslims have engaged in violent acts. To deny this would be as disingenuous as denying that Islam fundamentally embodies enlightened messages of harmony and that the overwhelming majority of Muslims live by principles of peace, compassion, and mercy.

The problem lies in the false dichotomy that is often presented: Islam is either peaceful or it's inherently violent. This binary narrative is both overly simplistic and misleading. The reality is that the Quran contains passages that speak to both peace and conflict. The existence of these dual injunctions is not unique to Islam and is not inherently problematic. The challenge, however, is in the interpretation and the selective emphasis on these teachings, which can be taken up by individuals or groups to serve their purposes. In this context, both non-violent and militant Muslims may feel justified in their actions or beliefs, as they may interpret the same texts in dramatically different ways. For some and few, the devotion to God is through the sword; for others and most, it is found through God's infinite and boundless mercy that peace is realized.

This complexity is not exclusive to Islam. Every major religion throughout history has faced similar challenges—texts and teachings that can be interpreted to justify both peace and violence. Therefore, as I explore these topics in this work, my focus will be on the themes of unbounded mercy, gratitude, and the peace that Islam offers as a way of life. That is where I believe the heart of the message lies.

However, it would be remiss not to address the broader issue of how all religions—Islam included—can be subjected to the same kinds of criticism, distortion, and manipulation. The media, political agendas, and societal narratives can shape the way religions are portrayed and understood. We have seen this repeatedly throughout history, where faiths have been weaponized or misrepresented to serve particular purposes, whether to incite fear, control populations or justify acts of aggression. Christianity, Judaism, Hinduism, Buddhism, and countless other creeds have faced similar distortions. The danger lies not in the religions themselves but in how certain elements can be taken out of context, misrepresented, or manipulated to promote divisive or violent agendas.

In this brief comparative analysis, my goal is to demonstrate that no religion is immune to these criticisms or manipulations. All faiths, when viewed through the lens of history or media, can be portrayed in ways that serve certain narratives, often at the expense of truth and understanding. Ultimately, it is up to individuals and communities to discern the deeper values of compassion, empathy, and peace that lie at the core of these spiritual teachings and to resist the urge to simplify or distort them for harmful purposes.

We could easily point to historical atrocities, such as the European Christians who migrated to the Americas, illegally seized land, and nearly exterminated an entire race of people—the Native Americans. We could recall the fact that priests accompanied soldiers during these conquests, often taking part in or endorsing acts of violence, murder, and torture against those who refused to convert to Christianity. One of the most chilling examples of such cruelty includes the deliberate distribution of blankets laced with smallpox to indigenous populations, an early form of biological warfare designed to decimate them. We could further highlight the justification of slavery by Christian slave owners, who grotesquely twisted their faith to rationalize the horrific treatment, dehumanization, and brutal punishment of slaves, all in the name of Christ. These are but a few examples of how Christianity has been implicated in violence and oppression throughout history.

There are currently Jewish people in 2024 who believe that the genocide that the Israeli regime is currently inflicting on the people of Palestine in Gaza has religious justification. For example, in some extreme interpretations, Palestinians are likened to Amalek, an ancient enemy of Israel mentioned in the Torah, whom the Israelites were commanded to destroy. Although most Jewish scholars and leaders reject such interpretations, some extremists use these analogies to justify violence and even ethnic cleansing. These groups represent a radical fringe of religious Zionism and hold views far removed from mainstream Judaism.

Even Buddhism—often regarded as the quintessential religion of peace, tolerance, and non-violence—has not been free from this pattern. For many, Buddhism is synonymous with compassion and non-harm, yet history reveals that violence has marred even this revered tradition. In recent memory, we have the tragic events of 2012 in Myanmar, where Buddhist monks either incited or directly ordered violence against the Rohingya Muslims. This persecution resulted in the deaths of thousands of Muslims and the forced displacement of over 700,000 people, many of whom fled their homes in search of safety and refuge. These acts of violence were not isolated incidents, and to this day, reports of atrocities, including ethnic cleansing and systematic persecution of the Rohingya, continue to emerge from Myanmar.

The fact of the matter is that in recent history, let's say the last 100 years, Muslims have faced the largest scale of violence and persecution—far more than any other religious group. Some studies show that upwards of two million Muslims have been killed due to the War on terror. Which appears to just be an attack on Muslim-majority countries...maybe we should just call it the War on Islam.

In all of these cases, whether they involve Muslims, Christians, Buddhists, or any other faith group, it would be both unfair and misguided to blame the religions themselves. Religion is not to blame for these acts of violence; rather, the fault lies with the individuals. Often, radical, power-hungry, or unevolved leaders will exploit these belief systems to incite violence, sow discord, or assert dominance for personal gain of power and money. Frequently, it is high-ranking clergy or influential figures who manipulate religious texts and teachings to justify or further their own twisted agendas, turning a message of peace into a weapon of oppression.

Those who control the media often appear to be the perpetrators in sowing discourse and have been instrumental in cultivating fear through biased narratives. There have been numerous acts of deadly violence committed in the West by individuals who either identified as Christian or had no clearly stated faith—but their religion was almost never placed at the center of the conversation.

Timothy McVeigh's bombing of the Oklahoma City federal building killed 168 people, yet his religious background was barely discussed. Anders Breivik, who described himself as a "cultural Christian," murdered 77 in Norway. Dylann Roof walked into a Black church and killed nine people. Patrick Crusius murdered 23 Hispanic shoppers in El Paso. Stephen Paddock killed 58 in Las Vegas. In none of these cases was their faith treated as defining or their religion put on trial.

Even in a long and violent history of Planned Parenthood attacks, the same pattern holds. Paul Hill, a former minister, murdered a doctor in Florida. Shelley Shannon, tied to the Army of God, bombed multiple clinics and tried to assassinate another physician. Eric Rudolph bombed the Olympics and a clinic in Atlanta. Robert Dear killed three people at a Planned Parenthood and called himself "a warrior for the babies." Each of these individuals either cited or was driven by Christian belief, yet media outlets almost never used the phrase *"Christian terrorism."*

But when a Muslim commits a violent act, the reaction is different. Islam is immediately brought forward. The headlines tie the religion to the act, the belief system is dissected, and the faith itself is condemned. The spotlight is rarely on the individual—it's placed squarely on the religion.

This double standard is not just inconsistent—it is unjust. It tells the world that some faiths will be judged by their highest teachings and others by their lowest moments. And it ensures that peace, no matter how often practiced by the majority, remains hidden beneath the noise of one man's atrocities.

These examples highlight a pattern: when perpetrators are non-Muslims, the media focuses on factors such as political ideology, mental health, or personal grievances while often downplaying or omitting their religious identity. In contrast, when the perpetrator is Muslim, their religion is emphasized, even when it is irrelevant to the crime.

Research supports this discrepancy. A study from Georgia State University found that terrorist attacks committed by Muslims receive 357% more media coverage than those by non-Muslims, suggesting a bias in reporting practices. Scholars have also noted that media representations often conflate Islam with terrorism, reinforcing stereotypes that unfairly associate Muslims with violence. This framing contributes to the spread of Islamophobic sentiments, perpetuating public perceptions of Muslims as inherently linked to terrorism.

The selective emphasis on a perpetrator's religion in media coverage reflects broader societal biases and reinforces harmful stereotypes. Balanced and comprehensive journalism is essential to providing context without stigmatizing entire communities based on the actions of individuals. By addressing these disparities, media outlets can play a crucial role in supporting understanding and reducing prejudice.

Candace Owens, an American political commentator and pundit, has publicly reflected on the treatment of Muslims following the events of September 11, 2001. In a discussion with George Janko, she addressed the mistreatment of Muslims after 9/11, acknowledging the challenges they faced during that period, and issued a public apology to Muslims. Additionally, in her podcast episode titled "What Really Happened on 9/11?" Owens delved into the aftermath of the attacks, discussing how fear and control tactics were employed, which led to widespread misconceptions about Muslims.

Whether it is the media controllers who have insidious motives, sensationalism, or cultural ignorance, it is futile to engage in a race to the bottom, stepping over one another to claim the moral high ground based on religious superiority. As an evolving and conscious species, we should rise above these divisions. We should strive to encourage, uplift, and support one another as fellow human beings, recognizing our shared humanity before all else. Education, empathy, and love should be the cornerstones of our interactions, and we should unite in standing against those who use religion as a tool for tyranny and violence.

Rather than allowing ourselves to be divided by manipulated narratives, we should come together to resist despots and tyrants, regardless of what religion or ideology they claim to represent. We have the resources, knowledge, and capacity to educate ourselves and others, to expose deception, and to shed light on the crimes being committed in the name of religion or God. In doing so, we can empower those who have been misled by these destructive leaders, helping them to see the truth and understand the depth of the manipulation they have been subjected to. We must strive to separate ideology from the behaviors of people or governments acting in the name of that ideology. Together, we can build a future where religion is a force for unity, peace, and love rather than division, violence, and hatred.

"What if the truth was never lost – just whispered too quietly for the world to hear?" –Ah Lee

Jesus (PBUH) in Islam

"I swear by the One who holds my soul—Jesus, the son of Mary, will return as a just ruler among you." –Prophet Muhammad

Few figures in human history hold the universal reverence and admiration that Jesus (PBUH) does. Across cultures, faiths, and traditions, he is seen as a beacon of spiritual wisdom, compassion, and righteousness. While Christianity upholds him as the central figure of divine grace, Islam also places him in the highest ranks of prophetic honor, considering him one of the greatest messengers of God. Many Christians worldwide also recognize Jesus (PBUH) as a prophet rather than God or the son of God and affirm his role as a messenger. His story is one of miracles, devotion, and unwavering faith, deeply intertwined with the message of monotheism (Tawhid) that echoes throughout the teachings of all prophets. Jesus (PBUH), in fact, is mentioned in the Quran more than Prophet Muhammad (PBUH).

In the Islamic tradition, Jesus (PBUH), or Isa ibn Maryam (Jesus, son of Mary), or in his native tongue, Aramaic, "Yeshua," is not merely a prophet but a divine sign of God's power and mercy. He is one of the five greatest messengers, alongside Noah, Abraham, Moses, and Muhammad (peace be upon them all), tasked with guiding humanity towards righteousness. His mission was to bring the Gospel as a confirmation of the Torah and to remind the Children of Israel of their covenant with God.

His life, from conception to ascension, is marked by miraculous events, each serving as a testament to the divine. Unlike ordinary men, Jesus' very birth was a miracle, and his life became a testimony of God's ability to manifest His will beyond human limitations.

Jesus' (PBUH) birth stands as one of the most profound moments in human history, one that defies the natural order yet remains entirely within God's supreme power. Born to the Virgin Mary (Maryam, PBUH), Jesus' arrival was a moment of divine intervention and mercy, a direct manifestation of God's creative power. The Quran narrates this miraculous event:

"She said, 'My Lord! How can I have a child when no man has touched me?' He said, 'This is how Allah creates what He wills. When He decrees a matter, He simply says to it, 'Be!' and it is." (Quran 3:47)

Maryam (PBUH), one of the most exalted women in Islamic tradition, was a model of piety, patience, and devotion. The entire chapter Surah Maryam (Chapter 19) in the Quran is dedicated to her story, an unparalleled honor reflecting her elevated status.

One of the staple Islamic beliefs about Jesus (PBUH) was that he was sent to restore pure monotheism, calling the Children of Israel back to the worship of the One True God. His teachings, as preserved in the Quran, emphasize compassion, humility, righteousness, and devotion to God—values that align seamlessly with Islam.

Muslims believe in the universality of God's messages and respect the prophets who came before Muhammad, acknowledging their contributions to spiritual and moral guidance. One of the remarkable shared beliefs between Islam and Christianity is a fundamental part of Islamic eschatology. Muslims believe that Jesus will return to earth during the End Times to fulfill his role in establishing justice.

The return of Jesus is seen as one of the pivotal events before the Day of Judgment. According to Islamic tradition, Jesus (PBUH) will descend to earth to defeat the false messiah, known as the Dajjal, and will then usher in of a time of peace and righteousness. This belief is rooted in the Quran, such as in Surah Az-Zukhruf (43:61), where it states: "And indeed, Jesus will be [a sign for] knowledge of the Hour, so be not in doubt of it, and follow Me. This is a straight path."

Jesus' return in Islam is closely linked with the establishment of truth and the ultimate triumph of good over evil. His role in Islamic eschatology serves as a powerful reminder of the shared spiritual heritage between Islam and Christianity, reinforcing the importance of unity, justice, and the divine purpose that transcends religious divides.

Jesus (PBUH) is not a figure of division but a symbol of unity. His life, teachings, and miracles remind us that faith transcends boundaries, that the search for truth is universal, and that in humility, prayer, and service to others, we find the divine.

THE BIRTH OF ISLAM

"It is in the numinous luminous that we discover our voluminous ruminous rhythms." –Ah Lee

Islam's history is rich, complex, and deeply influential, but this book does not aim to provide a detailed historical account. Instead, it focuses on the living essence of Islam—the practical and spiritual benefits it offers in the modern world. However, for those seeking a deeper exploration of the historical roots of Islam and the life of Prophet Muhammad (PBUH), I recommend *Muhammad: A Prophet for Our Time* by Karen Armstrong. Her work provides a well-researched, accessible, and engaging narrative of the Prophet's life and the early development of Islam, offering valuable insights into its historical and spiritual foundations. Included here is a very brief summary of the history of Islam:

Prophet Muhammad (PBUH), the central figure of Islam, was born in 570 CE in Mecca, a city revered for its religious significance but steeped in tribal rivalries and polytheistic worship. Orphaned as a child, he was raised by his uncle Abu Talib and earned a reputation for integrity, earning the title "Al-Amin" (The Trustworthy). He worked as a merchant and later married Khadija, a remarkable widow 15 years his senior, who not only supported him in his personal life but also became the first to believe in his divine mission. Khadija's unwavering faith and counsel provided Muhammad with strength during some of the most challenging periods of his life.

In 610 CE, while seeking solitude, fasting, and meditating in the Cave of Hira, Muhammad experienced a mystical encounter. The angel Gabriel appeared to him, commanding him to "read/recite." Which would later become the first revealed verses of the Quran. "Read in the Name of your Lord who created you. Created man from a clinging clot. Read! And your

Lord is Most Generous. Who taught by the pen, Taught Man what he did not know (Quran 96:1-5). Initially overwhelmed and distraught over the interaction, Muhammad found reassurance through Khadija, who recognized the divine nature of his experience and that it, in fact, was a message from God. This moment marked the beginning of the Quranic revelations, a series of divine messages that would continue for 23 years, guiding not only Muhammad but the course of history.

The early revelations emphasized monotheism, the equality of all humans before Allah, and social justice, challenging the entrenched inequalities and idol worship of Meccan society. Muhammad began preaching these messages to his closest companions, including Khadija, Ali ibn Abi Talib, Abu Bakr, and Zayd ibn Harithah. However, the Quraysh elites, fearing a threat to their power and economic interests, resisted violently. Muhammad and his followers endured persecution, boycotts, and exile, yet their faith and resilience grew stronger.

In 622 CE, as hostility in Mecca reached a peak, Muhammad and his followers migrated to Medina, an event known as the Hijra, which marks the beginning of the Islamic calendar. In Medina, Muhammad's leadership extended beyond spiritual matters; he united the city's diverse communities through the Constitution of Medina, which is often regarded as one of the first written constitutions in history, a groundbreaking charter that promoted coexistence and mutual respect among Muslims, other faiths and ethnicities. This period saw Islam evolve into a social, political, and spiritual force guided by principles of justice, compassion, and faith.

The Prophet's wisdom and strategic brilliance became evident in key events such as the Battle of Badr in 624 CE, where a small Muslim force triumphed over a much larger Meccan army, and the Battle of the Trench, where innovative tactics defended Medina against a coalition of enemies. These victories reinforced the legitimacy of Muhammad's mission and strengthened the growing Muslim community. In 630 CE, Muhammad and his followers entered Mecca peacefully, purifying the Kaaba of its idols and re-establishing it as a sanctuary dedicated to the worship of Allah. His clemency toward the Meccans, offering amnesty despite years of persecution, demonstrated the profound spiritual and moral values at the heart of Islam. Many embraced the faith, and by the time of his Farewell Pilgrimage in 632 CE, much of the Arabian Peninsula was united under Islam.

Prophet Muhammad's final sermon encapsulated the essence of his mission. He emphasized the oneness of Allah, the sanctity of life and property, and the equality of all believers, regardless of race or status. His teachings, rooted in love, justice, and submission to Allah, continue to inspire millions. Following his passing in 632 CE, his legacy was preserved in the Quran, regarded as the eternal word of Allah, and the Hadith, collections of his sayings and practices that guide Muslims in their daily lives.

The Quran's compilation began shortly after Muhammad's death when concerns arose about preserving its authenticity. Many Quran reciters had died in battles, notably at Yamama, prompting Abu Bakr, the first caliph, to commission Zayd ibn Thabit to collect the revelations into a single manuscript. During Uthman ibn Affan's caliphate, this compilation was standardized and distributed to key Islamic centers, ensuring the Quran's consistency across the rapidly expanding Muslim world. Today, the Quran remains unaltered, revered as the direct and unadulterated word of Allah.

The question of leadership after Muhammad's death led to the first major division in Islam. Some believed the successor should be chosen by consensus based on merit, while others argued that leadership was a divine right of the Prophet's family, specifically Ali ibn Abi Talib. This debate culminated in the selection of Abu Bakr as the first caliph, establishing the Sunni tradition of leadership through community consensus. Shia Muslims, however, upheld Ali as the rightful successor, viewing the Imamate as a divinely guided institution tied to the Prophet's lineage. This division deepened after the Battle of Karbala in 680 CE, where Husayn ibn Ali, the Prophet's grandson, was martyred. His sacrifice became a symbol of resistance to tyranny and is commemorated annually by Shia Muslims during Ashura.

Despite these divisions, Sunni and Shia Muslims share the core tenets of Islam, including belief in the oneness of Allah, the prophethood of Muhammad, and the Quran as divine revelation. Both traditions honor the spiritual, social, and moral teachings of the Prophet, emphasizing prayer, charity, and the pursuit of justice.

The story of Islam's beginnings is one of profound spiritual awakening, unwavering faith, and the unification of a fragmented society under principles of equality and devotion to Allah. Muhammad's life and teachings, coupled with the Quran's timeless guidance, have shaped a faith that continues to inspire billions of people worldwide. His legacy, both as a messenger of Allah and a leader of humanity, stands as a testament to the transformative power of faith and compassion.

"And hold firmly to the rope of Allah all together and do not become divided."
(Quran 3:103)

FIVE PILLARS OF ISLAM

Shahada, Salat, Zakat, Swan & Hajj

"Knowledge is the life of the mind." –Siddiq Abu Bakar

Islam is built upon a foundation of faith and practice, a structure designed to cultivate connection with the divine. At the core of this divine path stand the Five Pillars of Islam—fundamental acts of worship that guide a believer's relationship with Allah, the community, and the self. These pillars are not only rituals but spiritual anchors, aligning the soul with purpose and reinforcing a blueprint of devotion in daily life. Each pillar carries its own depth: Shahada (faith) affirms the oneness of God, salat (prayer) instills discipline and mindfulness, zakat (charity) purifies wealth and the heart, sawm (fasting) strengthens self-control and empathy, and hajj (pilgrimage) unites the believer with a legacy of submission and sacrifice. Together, they form a holistic path—one that integrates faith with action, belief with embodiment, and devotion with daily existence.

SHAHADA (FAITH)

"La ilaha illa Allah, Muhammadur Rasulullah."
(There is no God but God, and Prophet Muhammad is the messenger of God)

The shahada, the declaration of faith in Islam, holds profound significance for Muslims, embodying both spiritual and practical benefits. It serves as the profession of one's faith to God and His messenger, Prophet Muhammad (PBUH), marking a pivotal moment of acceptance and commitment to Islamic beliefs and practices.

One of Prophet Muhammad's (PBUH) most cherished teachings is the assurance that reciting the shahada for the first time, with true belief, expunges all past sins while preserving good deeds. This act of faith not only cleanses the soul but also establishes a deep connection with God, providing spiritual fulfillment and a sense of purpose.

Reciting the shahada signifies the acceptance of the oneness of God (Tawheed) and the submission to His will. This declaration is believed to be a pathway to salvation and forgiveness, offering hope for paradise in the afterlife.

Moreover, the shahada is a public proclamation of faith, welcoming individuals into the global community of Muslims, known as the ummah. This sense of belonging creates a supportive environment of brotherhood/sisterhood, providing strength and unity within the community.

As a guiding principle, the shahada shapes a Muslim's beliefs, actions, and moral conduct, offering a framework to lead a life in accordance with Islamic teachings. Embracing Islam and reciting the shahada is seen as a source of inner peace and contentment, providing a spiritual foundation that brings purpose and tranquility to life.

It's important to understand that the benefits of the shahada are deeply personal and can vary among individuals. Each person may experience and interpret these benefits in their own unique way, reflecting the profound and individual nature of faith in Islam.

SALAT (PRAYER)

"You pray in your distress and in your need: would that you might pray also in the fullness of your joy and in your days of abundance." –Khalil Gibran

Salat, the ritual prayer of Islam, is more than a routine act; it is the heartbeat of a Muslim's daily life and the most direct means of communion with Allah. Enjoined upon believers as an obligation and a source of spiritual purification, salat composes discipline, devotion, and mindfulness into the cadence of each day. This chapter begins by exploring the fundamental motions of prayer, allowing for a deeper understanding of its physical and spiritual dimensions. Additionally, we examine the physiological benefits of these movements, drawing comparisons to similar postures found in various physical disciplines, such as stretching and breath-centered exercises. Once the movements and their significance are clear, we will journey through the five daily prayers—fajr, zhuhr, asr, maghrib, and isha—each marking a divine appointment that segments time into periods of reflection and renewal. Finally, we will conclude with jumu'ah, the weekly congregational prayer that unites the community in collective worship.

Before we delve into the prayer itself, it is essential to first understand the preconditions that prepare us for this sacred engagement with our Lord. Much like one would meticulously prepare for an important interview, prayer requires a state of readiness—both physically and spiritually. Just as we take deliberate steps to present ourselves properly before a significant meeting, we must approach our Creator with the same reverence, ensuring that our hearts, minds, and bodies are aligned in devotion. This preparation is not merely a formality but a means of elevating our consciousness before standing in the presence of the divine.

Adhan (Call to Prayer)

"I was in India recently, and my hotel was near the Taj Mahal. Five times a day there would be a call for prayer, and it was the most beautiful thing. I was lying in my bed thinking no matter what your religion is, it would be great to have that reminder five times a day to remember your Lord and savior."
–Will Smith

The adhan (ah- dhan), commonly known as the call to prayer, is one of the most recognizable aspects of Islam. It is a rhythmic, melodious call that is recited aloud by a designated person called the mu'adhin (or muezzin in some regions), typically from a mosque's minaret. The purpose of the adhan is to announce the time of prayer and invite Muslims to join in worship. Five times a day, Muslims around the world hear this call, signaling that it is time for one of the five obligatory prayers. However, the adhan is not just a practical announcement; it is deeply spiritual, serving as a reminder for believers to pause and reconnect with the divine.

The words of the adhan are a proclamation of the fundamental beliefs in Islam: Below is the English translation and, as stated, is recited in a melodious and rhythmic manner.

God is the Greatest, God is the Greatest.

God is the Greatest, God is the Greatest.

I bear witness that there is no deity worthy of worship except God.

I bear witness that there is no deity worthy of worship except God.

I bear witness that Muhammad is the Messenger of God.

I bear witness that Muhammad is the Messenger of God.

Hasten to prayer.

Hasten to prayer.

Hasten to success.

Hasten to success.

God is the Greatest, God is the Greatest.

There is no deity worthy of worship except God.

This succinct, poetic form encapsulates the core tenets of the Islamic faith, acting as a reminder of the central role that prayer and submission to God play in a Muslim's life.

The origins of the adhan date back to the time of Prophet Muhammad (PBUH) in 7th-century Arabia. During the early years of Islam, the community sought a way to announce the time of prayer. After some discussion, the adhan was introduced, following a dream that one of the Prophet's companions had, in which he heard a voice calling people to prayer. The Prophet agreed that this was a divinely inspired method, and he entrusted Bilal ibn Rabah, a close companion and one of the earliest converts to Islam, to be the first mu'adhin. Bilal's voice, known for its deep resonance, carried the words of the adhan across the city of Medina, marking a historic moment for the Muslim community. His role became symbolic of the inclusivity and unity within Islam, as Bilal was a former slave who rose to prominence through his faith and devotion.

For Muslims, the adhan is not just an auditory signal but a spiritual call that transcends time and space. When the adhan is heard, it serves as a powerful reminder to step away from daily distractions and refocus on one's relationship with God. Responding to the adhan is, in itself, an act of worship, as it signifies a readiness to submit to the will of Allah and to engage in the sacred act of prayer. This moment offers a spiritual pause in the day, encouraging believers to reflect on their purpose and purify their intentions before standing in prayer.

The call to prayer resonates from mosques in cities, towns, and villages across the world, creating a shared experience among Muslims. No matter where one is, the sound of the adhan binds believers together in a global act of worship, transcending national and cultural boundaries. This collective call to prayer reinforces the unity of the Muslim ummah (community), reminding them that they are part of something greater than themselves— an international brotherhood bound by faith in the one true God.

For someone unfamiliar with the practice, the adhan might seem like a purely ritualistic call. However, it serves a far more meaningful purpose. It promotes mindfulness, encouraging Muslims to interrupt their daily routines and redirect their thoughts toward worship, humility, and submission to the Creator. The phrases of the adhan remind the listener not only of God's greatness but also of the transient nature of life and the eternal importance of spiritual growth. In this way, the adhan functions as both an external call to prayer and an internal invitation for self-reflection and spiritual cleansing.

A phenomenon that seems miraculous to me is that during every second of the day, the **adhan**—the sacred call to prayer—resonates somewhere on Earth, weaving a continuous thread of devotion under the coursing sun and watchful moon. As the dawn breaks and shadows stretch across the lands, Muslims in every corner of the world turn their hearts toward Allah in unison. When the call concludes in one region, it begins anew in another, creating an unbroken cycle of worship that mirrors the celestial journey of the heavens. This perpetual rhythm of faith is an immanent reminder of God's omnipresence and the unity of the global Muslim ummah. It is as if the adhan becomes the Earth's heartbeat, proclaiming the greatness of Allah with every passing second of every single day, 365 days a year, connecting believers in an eternal symphony of submission, gratitude, and peace. Such a phenomenon transcends human comprehension, standing as a wonderous testament to the universal and timeless nature of Islamic worship. I would like you to understand this completely: every second of the day, the adhan is being recited somewhere or another. Before the echo dies in one sky, it is born again in another.

The sound never stops. The miracle is not just that the adhan happens. The miracle is that it never stops.

The adhan is not just a call to prayer—it is a powerful spiritual summons that awakens the soul, calling believers to reconnect with their faith and their Creator. Its message transcends cultures and centuries, serving as a reminder of the core principles of Islam: faith in one God, unity, and submission to divine will. For Muslims and non-Muslims alike, the adhan offers a glimpse into the heart of Islamic worship, encouraging mindfulness, reflection, and a commitment to living a life of devotion, peace, and gratitude. Whether heard from a mosque in a bustling city or a quiet village, the adhan is a timeless invitation to rise above our temporal plane and engage with the infinite.

Ghusl (Ritual Bath)

Ghusl (ghoo-suhl), known in Islamic terminology as the "ritual bath" or "major ablution," is a sacred religious practice that symbolizes both physical and metaphysical purification. Unlike routine bathing, ghusl is carried out with specific ritualistic actions and a conscious intention, "niyyah" (nee-yah), to cleanse not only the body but also the soul. This sacred act transcends mere hygiene, reflecting the importance of purity in the Islamic faith. It aligns with the broader Islamic principle of "taharah" (tah-ha-rah), or ritual purity, which prepares the individual for acts of worship such as prayer, handling the Quran, and other spiritual activities.

While ghusl has parallels in other religious practices, such as the **tvilah** in Judaism, the Christian practice of **baptism**, and Hindu pilgrims bathing in the Ganges, it remains distinct in its requirements and the occasions for its performance. Ghusl is obligatory under specific circumstances, including after sexual intercourse, ejaculation, menstruation, childbirth, and the cessation of postpartum bleeding. Beyond these mandatory occasions, it is also highly recommended before significant congregational prayers, such as the jumu'ah prayer or the eid prayers, as well as after washing a deceased body, reflecting the importance of both personal and communal purity in Islam.

The physical actions of ghusl are straightforward but deeply symbolic. It involves making the intention to God to accept and cleanse you physically and spiritually, then washing the entire body, ensuring that every inch of the skin is cleansed in a specific sequence. Water, in this context, serves as both a physical cleanser and a symbol of spiritual purification. Muslims believe that through the act of washing, not only are dirt and physical impurities removed, but also the spiritual stains of sin. This is a moment of renewal and rebirth, where the individual can metaphorically shed the burdens of their past transgressions and emerge in a state of elevated consciousness, ready to re-engage with the divine.

Beyond the immediate religious requirements, ghusl has broader psychological, emotional, and physiological benefits. For many, it acts as a reset button, promoting mental clarity and emotional balance. The act of cleansing, combined with the sacred intention, creates an atmosphere of serenity, calmness, and self-reflection. As the physical dirt washes away, so do negative thoughts and emotions, allowing the individual to approach their acts of worship with a pure heart and mind. This can also lead to deeper self-discipline and spiritual growth, reinforcing the individual's commitment to their faith and personifies a stronger connection with God.

From a historical perspective, ghusl was a revolutionary practice in the Arabian Peninsula during the early days of Islam. At a time when hygiene standards were not universally emphasized, Islam's requirement for regular bodily purification set the faith apart and elevated its spiritual discipline. This emphasis on cleanliness is in line with the Prophet Muhammad's (PBUH) teaching that "cleanliness is half of faith" (Sahih Muslim). Ghusl, therefore, carries an intrinsic connection to the Islamic ethos of cleanliness and purity, both externally and internally.

These rituals encourage self-reflection and mindfulness, creating an environment for personal growth and introspection. These acts, across various religions, represent a human yearning for renewal and transformation, where water becomes the conduit for elevation and purification.

Wudu (Ritual Ablution)

Complementing ghusl is the practice of wudu (woo-doo), the Islamic ritual of purification involving the washing of specific body parts. The process typically includes washing the hands, mouth, nose, face, and arms up to the elbows, wiping the head and ears, and washing the feet up to the ankles in a specific sequence. While ghusl purifies the entire body, wudu focuses on cleansing specific parts and is performed before each prayer every time. Though the physical scope of wudu is narrower than ghusl, its spiritual and symbolic weight is no less significant. Wudu is an act of spiritual readiness, allowing the individual to enter a state of purity before approaching Allah in prayer.

The primary purposes of wudu is to cultivate mindfulness and prepare the worshiper for direct communication with their Creator. By engaging in the physical act of washing away impurities, the individual also mentally purifies themselves, focusing their thoughts on the forthcoming prayer. This transition from worldly distractions to divine focus mirrors the Islamic view of prayer as an opportunity to realign one's life with spiritual and ethical ideals.

Physiologically, wudu also carries benefits that extend beyond its spiritual purpose. By regularly washing the hands, face, and other exposed areas, wudu promotes personal hygiene and cleanliness. This is particularly important given the frequency with which wudu is performed—five times a day before each prayer. This repetitive cleansing has health benefits, such as reducing the spread of germs and preventing infections. For example, rinsing the mouth and nose multiple times a day helps clear away harmful bacteria, thus contributing to improved oral hygiene.

Furthermore, the act of washing and massaging various body parts during wudu can enhance blood circulation, promoting oxygen delivery to the skin and tissues. Regular performance of wudu also serves as a stress reliever, providing moments of calm and reflection throughout the day. This is especially important in modern society, where constant stimuli and stressors can take a toll on mental health. By engaging in wudu, Muslims are reminded to pause, reflect, and focus on their spiritual well-being.

Wudu's importance is also reflected in Islamic teachings regarding the cleanliness of the heart and mind. By purifying the body through wudu, Muslims believe that they are also preparing their souls to be in a state of humility and submission to Allah. This underscores the dual purpose of wudu: it serves both as a physical act of hygiene and as a spiritual exercise that deepens the individual's connection to their faith.

From a modern perspective, wudu may also hold relevance in combating some of the health challenges of the digital age. For instance, exposure to electromagnetic fields (EMFs) from electronic devices is a growing concern. The repetitive cleansing involved in wudu may help the body neutralize or rid itself of these subtle but potentially harmful electromagnetic charges, aligning with Islamic teachings that emphasize the importance of cleanliness not only for ritual purity but also for health and well-being. Water helps ground the negative charges that our skin may be holding on to. Also, it is worth noting that the CDC recommendation for those exposed to radiation is as follows: If a shower isn't available, At a sink or faucet, wash your hands, face, and any exposed skin using plenty of water. Pay special attention to your hands and face, and gently blow your nose and wipe your eyelids, eyelashes, and ears. These are literally the steps in performing wudu.

The variation in how wudu is practiced among different Islamic cultures and sects adds richness to this already profound ritual. While the core principles remain consistent, certain cultural adaptations reflect the diversity of the Muslim world. Whether in America, Africa, the Middle East, or Southeast Asia, wudu is universally recognized as a necessary act of purification, yet its slight differences reflect the beauty of Islamic diversity.

Wudu is believed to cleanse not only the physical body but also the bioenergetic field, often referred to as the aura in spiritual and metaphysical traditions. A preliminary study using Resonant Field Imaging (RFI) found that after performing wudu, participants exhibited notable enhancements in their energy field, with a majority showing improvements in the head, throat, and limb regions (Alias et al., 2011). This aligns with the idea that water, a natural conductor, may help discharge excess electromagnetic buildup and rebalance the body's bioelectrical state, much like grounding (earthing) does. Metaphysical traditions describe the aura as an energetic reflection of one's mental, emotional, and spiritual condition, and wudu—through its repetitive act of washing and focused intention—may serve as both a biophysical and metaphysical reset (Alias et al., 2011). While the concept of the aura remains scientifically unconfirmed, research in biophotons and bioelectromagnetic fields suggests that the body emits subtle energy, which can be influenced by environmental and physiological factors. In this way, wudu acts as a harmonization of the body's energetic state, fostering relaxation, mental clarity, and an elevated spiritual presence—bridging the gap between metaphysical purification and physiological well-being.

Lastly, wudu also serves as a reminder of the importance of self-discipline and spiritual mindfulness. The act of cleansing oneself before each prayer cultivates an awareness of one's actions, intentions, and spiritual state. It is a practice that emphasizes consistency, reminding Muslims to approach their day with a clean heart, mind, and body.

Together, ghusl and wudu form an integrated approach to purification in Islam. While ghusl is an in-depth renewal of spiritual and physical purity, wudu acts as a frequent touchstone that brings believers back to their center throughout the day. Both acts emphasize that purification is not only about the physical body but about cultivating a clean and mindful approach to one's spiritual life.

Equally important is awrah "ow-rah" coverage or proper dress, which embodies modesty and reverence for the act of worship. Men are required to cover from the navel to the knees, while women must cover their entire body, including the head, except for the face, hands, and feet, mirroring the modest attire of nuns who symbolize purity and humility in their devotion to God. This practice is not merely a physical covering but a spiritual act of concealing distractions and presenting oneself before the Creator with dignity and respect.

Another precondition before salat begins with niyyah "nee-yah" (intentionality of prayer), where the heart must align solely with the purpose of worship, ensuring sincerity in devotion to Allah. This sacred act should be performed as a heartfelt offering to the creator. Together, these elements elevate salat beyond a ritual, transforming it into a sacred journey of the heart and soul toward Allah.

Sacred Alignments: The Sajjadah, Kaaba, and Qiblah

When Muslims pray, they often use a prayer mat called a sajjadah (saj-jah-dah). The sajjadah serves as a clean, sacred space for worship, often adorned with intricate geometric designs and symbolic motifs. These designs frequently feature representations of a mihrab (an architectural niche found in mosques, indicating the direction of prayer) or elements inspired by the Kaaba (Kaa-bah).

The Kaaba, located at the heart of the Masjid al-Haram (the Sacred Mosque) in Mecca, Saudi Arabia, is revered as the holiest site in Islam. This cube-shaped structure is the focal point of Muslim prayer, a practice known as facing the qiblah (kib-lah), or direction of prayer. The orientation of the Kaaba is remarkable, as it aligns very well with the cardinal directions—

north, south, east, and west—a testament to advanced astronomical knowledge and meticulous planning in ancient times.

One of the most iconic features of the Kaaba is the Black Stone, a small, sacred rock embedded in one of its corners. While it holds great historical and religious significance, it is important to understand that Muslims do not worship the stone. It is venerated as a blessed relic, symbolizing a connection to Prophet Muhammad (PBUH) and the traditions of Islam. During pilgrimage, some Muslims strive to touch or kiss the stone, emulating the Prophet's example, though this act is neither obligatory nor central to worship.

The Kaaba represents the unity of the global Muslim ummah (community), as millions face this sacred structure in prayer each day. However, it is essential to note that Muslims do not worship the Kaaba itself; it serves solely as a unifying direction and a symbol of devotion to Allah.

The Kaaba's significance dates back to the earliest days of monotheism. According to Islamic belief, it was originally built by Prophet Adam, the first human and prophet. Over time, the structure fell into disrepair and was later rebuilt by Prophet Abraham (Ibrahim) and his son Ishmael (Ismail) as a sanctuary for the worship of the one true God. This event marked the Kaaba's restoration as a spiritual center and the establishment of rituals such as tawaf (tah-wahf), or circumambulation, performed during pilgrimage.

In the pre-Islamic era, the Kaaba became a site of polytheistic worship, housing idols representing various deities. However, upon the conquest of Mecca, Prophet Muhammad (PBUH) restored its sanctity by removing the idols and rededicating the Kaaba to Allah alone. Interestingly, historical accounts suggest that the Prophet spared certain depictions, including a painting of Mary and Prophet Jesus (Isa) (PBUH) and a fresco of Prophet Abraham (Ibrahim), emphasizing Islam's respect for shared prophetic heritage.

Throughout history, the Kaaba has undergone several renovations and restorations, with its current structure dating back to 952 CE. Despite these changes, its simplicity and antiquity remain profound symbols of the enduring relationship between the Creator and His creation. For Muslims, the Kaaba stands as a timeless reminder of unity, faith, and the eternal presence of Allah.

Prayer Positions and Postures

The body is a vessel of devotion, and movement is its unspoken language of surrender. In salat, each posture is not just a motion but an expression—of humility, alignment, and submission. Across cultures and disciplines, structured movement has long been used to cultivate focus, discipline, and breath awareness. While salat remains unique in its divine purpose, its physical postures share physiological benefits with other structured movement practices, such as yoga, Qigong, and breath-centered disciplines. This section explores these similarities purely from a physical and biomechanical perspective, without borrowing external spiritual connotations, reinforcing the wisdom embedded in the natural design of prayer. While I describe the prayer positions and postures with as much accuracy as possible, please note that variations exist across different schools of thought and cultures, and any errors are unintentional.

The physical movements in salat—standing (qiyaam), bowing (ruku), prostration (sujood), and sitting (julus)—are more than external expressions; they mirror the flow of energy within the body. From a personal perspective, the practice of daily salat has revealed its similarities to Taoist spiritual disciplines—not just in form but in essence.

Though their purposes remain distinct, mindfulness, self-discipline, and inner peace are central to Taoist practice and salat. Just as Taoist practitioners cultivate awareness through breath and presence, prayer instills a profound sense of mindfulness. Every movement, word, and moment in salat demands full presence, clearing mental clutter and anchoring the soul.

Likewise, self-discipline is a core tenet in both traditions; Taoism speaks of aligning one's actions with the natural order rather than resisting it, while prayer trains the soul to move in synchrony with divine will, refining discipline and consistency. Ultimately, clarity and inner peace arise when one ceases inner resistance—a key teaching in Taoist philosophy. In the same way, salat instills inner serenity, removing the dissonance caused by worldly distractions and replacing it with divine tranquility. In both traditions, spiritual discipline is not about force but about flow—a surrender that is not defeat but liberation.

Qiyam   Namaste

When first coming to your prayer, you must make niyyah (nee-yah). Niyyah is the quiet intention in your heart for God to accept your prayers). Takbir (tak-beer) is the beginning of the prayer and starts by facing the qiblah (the direction of Mecca that all Muslims face during prayer) and raising both hands next to the ears and reciting, "Allahu Akbar" (God is great). Next, assume the position of qiyaam by standing straight and lowering your hands at your sides or crossed in front of you, just above your navel. Depending on your school of thought or tradition. Both positions, from a physical standpoint, have their own unique benefits and allow for a calm focus (both Sunni and Shia practices acknowledge this).

The qiyaam position is reminiscent of the samasthiti or tadasana pose from traditional yoga. This practice is designed to increase physical energy through a posture of stillness. Although it may seem surprising that standing still can yield health benefits, practitioners of *yoga* attest to significant improvements in energy levels, and it is akin to the stillness of qiyaam.

Whether you are practicing salat or qigong or even yoga, these standing, upright, relaxed postures have significant health benefits.

- Reduced strain on the neck, shoulders, and back.

- Engaging core muscles, strengthening the legs, and improving physical balance and coordination.
- Reduced strain on joints and improved flexibility in the knees, hips, and ankles, alleviating stiffness over time.
- Physically aligning the body improves oxygenation and blood flow and boosts energy and vitality.
- Stillness of both practices cultivates concentration, reduces mental chatter, and encourages mindfulness.
- Qiyaam strengthens spiritual connection through prayer, while tadasana aligns the body's energy, called Qi, promoting inner harmony.
- Relaxation and focus reduce stress, enhance sleep quality, and help calm the mind.
- Regular standing practice offsets the negative effects of prolonged sitting, such as stiffness, reduced circulation, and fatigue.

Once you have recited the required prayer, you will briefly raise your hands to the side of your head next to the ears and say "Allahu Akbar" and then prepare to transition into the ruku position.

Ruku / Ardha Uttanasana

Ruk'u   Ardha Uttanasana

The second movement in a prayer is ruku, where you bow forward, placing both hands on your knees. In yoga, this position parallels *ardha uttanasana*, also known as the half-forward bend. This posture is meant to lengthen the spine and fold the torso over the legs, much like the Islamic ruku, but with slight modifications. In yoga, the arms may reach toward the floor or rest on the back of the legs, whereas in ruku, the hands remain steady on the knees.

The benefits of ruku or *ardha uttanasana* are numerous:

- A gentle stretch to the hamstrings improves flexibility and relieves tension in the muscles.
- Spinal lengthening and decompression, which counteracts the effects of prolonged sitting and improves posture.
- A gentle release of tightness in the lower back and shoulders, offering a soothing stretch that promotes relaxation.
- Mild compression of the abdomen, stimulating digestion and aiding in relieving digestive discomfort.
- Stress relief and mental clarity, as the forward-folding motion calms the mind and encourages focus.

- The act of bowing also encourages mindfulness and grounding and can contribute to increased circulation and an energy boost.

Both ruku and *ardha uttanasana* emphasize humility and surrender. The physical posture mirrors the spiritual intention of bowing to the divine, whether in the context of Islam or the discipline of yoga. However, while yoga emphasizes the physical and philosophical benefits, Islamic ruku is an act of worship and humility, surrendering to God in prayer. Once you recite the required prayer in the ruku position you will then return to qiyaam and again briefly raise your hands to your ears and say" Allahu Akbar" and prepare to transition into the position of Sujud.

Sujud / Balasana / Child's Pose

Sujud   Balasana

The next posture is sujud, the act of prostration. Sujud involves kneeling and touching your forehead to the ground. In yoga, a similar pose is the balasana or child's pose. Sujud, like balasana, is a moment of complete surrender—both physically and spiritually. The palms are placed on the ground beside the head, with the forehead touching your prayer mat or the earth. For Shia Muslims, they rest their foreheads on a piece of clay called a *mohr*, symbolizing a connection to the earth.

The benefits of sujud, which are similar to those of balasana, include:

- The gentle decompression of the spine relieves tension and improves posture.
- Stretching of the lower back, hips, thighs, and ankles, reducing stiffness.
- Gentle abdominal compression aids digestion and alleviates bloating.
- Releasing the chest and shoulders helps ease tension in the upper back and neck.
- Increases blood flow to the brain, enhancing oxygenation and mental clarity.

- Activation of the parasympathetic nervous system, promoting relaxation and inner peace.
- Spiritual submission and surrender.
- Mindfulness and emotional balance.
- Grounding to restore stability and revitalization.

Both sujud and balasana share many physical, mental, and spiritual benefits, making them valuable practices for holistic well-being. After completing sujud, you transition into the julus position.

Julus / Seiza / Vajrasana

Julus   Seiza

Similar to the traditional Japanese way of sitting, called *seiza,* and the yoga posture *vajrasana*, the Islamic prayer posture julus requires the individual sits on their heels, with the buttocks resting lightly on the ankles with hands resting comfortably on the thighs or knees. The term *seiza* translates to "correct sitting" in Japanese and is deeply rooted in practices such as meditation, traditional tea ceremonies, and martial arts. Similarly, *vajrasana* is often employed in yoga for meditation and pranayama (breathing exercises). Both postures, like *julus*, are designed to promote a sense of groundedness, balance, and calmness.

You then return to sujud briefly and recite a few more lines of prayer before resuming qiyaam—the standing position. This completes a cycle known as a *rakat* (qiyaam—ruku—qiyaam—sujud—julus—sujud—julus). Shia Muslims will complete their prayers saying "God is great, God is great, God is great" whilst raising their hands to their head close to the ears in the position of julus in three consecutive motions. Sunni Muslims complete their prayers in the Salam position, which involves turning their head to the right and left while reciting "Peace and mercy of Allah be upon you." And I believe most Muslims will go back to Sujud for one last prostration to their lord with their head to the ground and pray for the things in their heart.

In the context of prayer, *julus* transcends its physical form, embodying a moment of reflection, humility, and spiritual connection. It is a time to recite supplications or *du'a*, reinforcing the practitioner's focus on their relationship with the divine. This stillness creates a bridge between the active motions of prayer and the contemplative pauses within it.

The benefits of sitting in this position are both physical and mental, as evidenced by practices that emphasize seated meditation or grounded postures. Some notable benefits include:

- A straight spine to help correct poor posture and support a healthy musculoskeletal structure.
- Reduces strain on the back and shoulders.
- Facilitates deep breathing, allowing the diaphragm to move freely and promoting greater oxygen intake. Mindful breathing enhances focus and a sense of tranquility.
- Promotes flexibility in the knees, ankles, and hips. Over time, it may also help prevent stiffness or joint discomfort.
- Improved blood circulation, particularly in the lower extremities, aiding in reducing fluid retention.
- The grounded, stable nature of the posture encourages concentration and mindfulness. Whether in meditation, martial arts, or prayer, this position provides a sense of rootedness, anchoring the mind and body in the present moment.

For those unaccustomed to sitting in julus or seiza, the posture may initially feel challenging. However, regular practice fosters a sense of patience, resilience, and discipline, qualities that are integral to both spiritual growth and personal development.

While the benefits are extensive, it is important to recognize that this posture may not be comfortable for everyone, particularly individuals with knee, ankle, or hip issues. Modifications or alternative seated positions can be adopted to ensure inclusiveness while preserving the essence of humility and stillness inherent in this practice.

Ultimately, the julus position serves as a powerful reminder of the union between the physical and spiritual, grounding the practitioner both physically and emotionally in the act of prayer and contemplation.

The physical movements of prayer are not just rituals; they are expressions of spiritual alignment, embodying humility, discipline, and presence. Just as yogic philosophy teaches the importance of breath-linked movement to achieve mindfulness with the natural order, the positions of salat guide the body and mind into a harmonized state of surrender. Each movement—standing, bowing, prostrating, and sitting—is a deliberate act of balance between stillness and motion, submission and intention, form and essence. In Taoism, true alignment is not found in resisting form but in flowing with the rhythm of existence. Likewise, the positions of Islamic prayer—though divinely prescribed—are not burdens imposed upon the body but sacred movements designed to realign it. Each posture invites the soul to release control, ground the self, quiet the ego, and surrender to a higher harmony. The structure becomes the flow, and within it, the heart learns to move with God.

Yet, these postures are only the vessel—what fills them with meaning is prayer itself. The sacred act of standing before God in fajr, the quiet solitude of where the body's alignment transforms into spiritual awakening. With each prayer throughout the day, these positions become gateways to presence, reflection, and divine connection. Now, let us step into the essence of salat itself—beginning with the first light of the morning, fajr.

Fajr (Morning Prayer)

"Put God first! Put God first in everything that you do!"
–Denzel Washington

Fajr (fah-jr) is the first of the five obligatory daily prayers in Islam. It consists of two rakats performed at dawn before the sun rises. It holds immense significance, as it marks the beginning of the day with devotion and a deep spiritual connection to God. Each of the five daily prayers is tied to specific times of the day based on the movement of the sun, which varies by geographical location and season. The fajr prayer signifies the transition from night to day, providing a unique opportunity to seek guidance, offer thanks, and ask for protection as one embarks on the day's journey.

Once wudu (the ritual washing) is performed, the believer stands facing the Kaaba, the sacred house in Mecca, and begins the prayer. Facing the qibla—the direction toward the Kaaba—is a unifying act for Muslims around the globe, symbolizing the shared worship of one God. The fajr prayer not only serves as a spiritual reminder of this unity but also allows believers to start their day by turning to God in humble submission, asking for guidance, mercy, and strength to face life's challenges.

The pre-dawn hours are seen as particularly blessed in Islam, a time when the world is still and the heart is most receptive. This serene atmosphere offers the ideal conditions for self-reflection, introspection, and seeking forgiveness from Allah. Many believers find that performing the fajr prayer brings an inner peace that carries throughout the day, fortifying them with spiritual clarity and resilience. Waking up for fajr is a practice of discipline and self-control, qualities that extend beyond prayer into daily life, instilling habits of punctuality and perseverance.

Additionally, Muslims believe that starting the day with the fajr prayer invites blessings (barakah) into their lives. These blessings can manifest as greater success in their endeavors, clearer decision-making, and overall well-being. Research even supports the notion that early risers benefit from better physical and mental health. Studies from institutions such as the University of Colorado Boulder, MIT, and Harvard have shown that people who wake up early tend to enjoy better sleep quality and a lower risk of depression. Further studies have indicated that early risers often experience improved health and happiness, with a greater ability to focus and achieve their goals. A study published in *Nature Communications* (Daghlas et al., 2019) found that individuals with a genetic predisposition to waking up early reported greater well-being and a reduced risk of depression. Furthermore, research in *JAMA Psychiatry* (Daghlas et al., 2021) demonstrated that waking up just one hour earlier can lower the risk of major depression by 23%.

The fajr prayer is much more than a mere religious obligation. It is a deep soulful practice that offers benefits for the body, mind, and soul. By rising early to pray, Muslims invite blessings into their day, fortify themselves with divine guidance, and cultivate an attitude of gratitude that positively impacts their emotional and psychological well-being. Whether through the spiritual connection forged with Allah or the physical benefits accrued from regular prayer, the significance of fajr extends far beyond the moment of prayer itself. It is a timeless practice that continues to inspire, guide, and uplift millions of Muslims around the world every single day.

The fajr prayer can take around five to seven minutes to complete. It serves as a disciplined way to start the day, offering spiritual grounding, mild physical stretches, and increased blood flow. By performing this prayer, you not only fulfill a religious obligation but also give yourself time for reflection and gratitude. I myself use this moment to validate my personal goals and desires. For instance, after the *fajr* or *isha* prayers, I like to spend an additional 15–30 minutes meditating, offering gratitude, reflecting on my goals, breathing, and reaffirming my personal affirmations. This provides me with an extra opportunity for introspection, free from the distractions of technology and otherworldly disturbances, and is also deeply rejuvenating. As I often say, Islamic prayer is not simply an obligation but a beneficial practice for the mind, body, and soul.

For me personally, being an early riser has deepened my appreciation for the fajr prayer. Though I won't dive into the specific recitations of the prayers or variations among the Islamic sects, I believe the essence of the prayer—worship, gratitude, and submission to God—transcends these differences. To me, it's less about the details and more about the intention and connection we make during prayer. If you wish to explore the precise Islamic prayer, translations of Islamic prayers, and prayer motions and movements, I invite you to consult the World Wide Web, which should have thousands of resources for you.

Zuhur (Midday Prayer)

Zuhur (zoo-hur) is observed after midday and is comprised of four rakats. While it may appear to some as a disruption to a busy workday, it offers a unique opportunity to enhance productivity, reduce stress, and regain focus.

In the midst of life's daily demands, taking a brief pause for zuhur provides a vital moment for introspection, gratitude, and spiritual connection. This prayer encourages us to take a step back from the hustle and bustle of life, allowing us to recenter ourselves and realign our focus on the greater purpose. Moreover, performing the ritual of wudu before prayer not only cleanses the body of physical impurities but also helps clear the mind and reduce exposure to electromagnetic static accumulated from various electronic devices throughout the day. The act of washing before prayer, paired with the physical movements during the prayer, stimulates blood circulation and encourages mental and physical rejuvenation.

Zuhur prayer is not just an act of worship; it embodies discipline, balance, and time management. When we prioritize our spiritual duties alongside worldly responsibilities, it leads to a more structured, balanced approach to life. Instead of viewing zuhur as an interruption, we can see it as an essential mental break, a much-needed pause to reset, gain clarity, and cultivate inner peace.

The benefits of this midday prayer resonate beyond the spiritual realm. According to research, mental breaks—such as naps, meditation, or walks in nature—enhance productivity, replenish attention, and improve memory and creativity. In this context, zuhur provides an ideal mental and physical break, offering not only spiritual fulfillment but also increased efficiency and creativity as we return to our daily tasks.

As the Zen proverb wisely advises, "You should sit in meditation for twenty minutes every day—unless you're too busy. Then you should sit for an hour." Such moments of stillness and connection, like those we experience during zuhur, allow us to remain grounded and better equipped to handle life's demands. By incorporating these mindful breaks into our routines, we instill greater resilience, productivity, and a deeper sense of purpose.

Asr (Late Afternoon Prayer)

The asr (ah-sir) prayer, performed in the late afternoon, holds its valid time from midway between noon and sunset. Asr is a prayer that invites reflection, humility, and a plea for forgiveness and mercy, reminding us of the fleeting nature of life and the importance of spiritual sustenance amidst worldly responsibilities.

Some Muslims (specifically Shia prefer to combine zuhur and asr prayers. But there is some debate within the Islamic community regarding the validity of combining prayers, with different sects holding differing views. However, from my perspective, prayers should ideally be performed at their prescribed times, as dictated by the adhan (call to prayer) according to one's local time zone. If one's circumstances allow, I believe it's beneficial and proper to perform prayers separately, respecting the set time for each adhan. Yet, for individuals, especially professionals with demanding schedules, combining prayers may be more practical and equally valid in many situations.

Asr consists of four rakats and requires the performance of wudu, allowing you to cleanse yourself of any impurities accumulated since your previous prayer. This not only refreshes the body but also offers a few more precious moments for stillness, gratitude, and reflection. As with all daily prayers, asr is an opportunity to recenter, realign, and reconnect with the divine, giving you a break from the busyness of the day, while also fostering a sense of inner peace, movement, and mental clarity.

Maghrib (Sunset Prayer)

Beginning right after sunset, maghrib (magh-rib) consists of three rakats. For many working professionals, this prayer often aligns with the time they return home, reuniting with their families. Before commencing the prayer, wudu (ablution) is once again performed, offering the chance to cleanse oneself of the day's impurities, both physical and spiritual, and prepare to enter into a state of worship.

Maghrib represents the transition from daylight to darkness, symbolizing the passage of time and the end of the day's labor. It serves as a reminder of life's fleeting nature and the importance of utilizing each moment to draw nearer to Allah. In this brief but meaningful period, For those fasting during Ramadan, maghrib also marks the time to break the fast, creating an especially poignant connection between the physical act of nourishment and the spiritual sustenance provided by prayer.

For families, this prayer can be a beautiful opportunity to come together in worship. It provides a moment to pause, recenter, and refocus on the family unit while reflecting on the blessings of home and togetherness. The significance of maghrib can vary from person to person, depending on their individual spiritual journey and devotion. Yet, at its core, maghrib serves as a time to relax, realign with faith, and express gratitude for the day that has passed.

Isha (Night Prayer)

Isha is the final prayer of the day, performed after the twilight has disappeared and before midnight. Consisting of four rakats, isha marks the completion of the five daily prayers and symbolizes the conclusion of one's spiritual duties for the day. Isha is a moment for ruminous thoughts, a time to seek forgiveness, offer supplications, and reflect on the day that has passed. It emphasizes the believer's devotion and discipline toward God and serves as a reminder of the trust placed in Allah's care and protection throughout the night.

This prayer also signifies the preparation for rest and sleep as they seek Allah's refuge from harm, evil, and negative influences that may emerge during the night. It's a moment to find tranquility and peace before bedtime, offering not only a spiritual experience but also a gentle stretch, relaxation, and re-centering after the day's activities.

As previously mentioned, I personally dedicate an additional 15 to 30 minutes of meditation following fajr in the morning and isha at night. This quiet time allows me to clear my mind, focus on my breathing, and engage in gratitude. It's a period to reflect on the day and visualize the things I wish to manifest, whether from within myself or from the greater universe—the Infinite, the Lord. This regular practice of reflection and meditation helps me maintain a sense of calm and intention before sleep, enhancing my spiritual connection and overall well-being.

Juma (Friday Congregation)

Juma is the Friday midday prayer that replaces zuhur and is performed in congregation, typically at a mosque. For Muslims unable to attend a mosque, it is often prayed in groups, bringing together families, friends, and local communities. Friday holds a special place in Islamic tradition, being considered the holiest day of the week—akin to a sabbath—and juma is viewed as a central act of worship and community gathering.

The juma prayer is obligatory for all adult males, except in certain conditions where attendance may not be possible. Historically, juma has deep cultural and religious significance. Some scholars point to its roots in pre-Islamic Arabian market days, when communities would gather on Fridays. Others note the influence of the Jewish and Christian sabbath in the institutionalization of juma in the Islamic tradition. It serves as a day of spiritual renewal, congregation, and remembrance of Allah, encouraging a sense of unity and collective worship among Muslims worldwide.

The Physical and Mental Benefits of Prayer

Dhikr (Remembrance of God) is one of the simplest yet most profound spiritual tools in Islam. Repetitive recitation of divine names and supplications aligns closely with the principles of mantra meditation as well as breath-centered practices in Taoism. Similarly in Sufi traditions, Dhikr is often performed with conscious breathwork. The Prophet Muhammad (PBUH) said: *"Verily, in the remembrance of Allah do hearts find peace."* (Quran 13:28)

This aligns deeply with Taoist teachings on inner stillness—just as one aligns with the Tao through presence, a Muslim attains spiritual clarity through constant remembrance of the divine.

The physical movements performed during the prayer are more than acts of devotion. They also have been shown to offer several physical health benefits. A 2018 study published in the *Journal of Bodywork and Movement Therapies* found that the repetitive motions involved in Islamic prayer can improve flexibility, balance, and range of motion. Another study from 2020 showed that these movements help with spine curvature and posture, contributing to overall physical health. Additionally, a 2019 study from the *Journal of Religion and Health* found that prayer movements could improve joint flexibility and muscle strength.

Beyond the physical benefits, numerous studies have shown that prayer and gratitude—key components of prayer—can positively impact mental health. For instance, McCullough et al. (2002) found a strong correlation between gratitude and overall life satisfaction, optimism, and happiness. "Gratitude is the stem cell of all worship" (David Roher). Gratitude helps individuals reframe their perspective, reducing feelings of victimhood and resentment. I am emphasizing gratitude because worship and gratitude are semantically related. In some cases, you can use "worship" instead of the noun "gratitude," especially in the context of religious acts. In the words of Dr. Jordan B. Peterson, a clinical psychologist, "There is great utility in gratitude. It also protects against the dangers of victimhood and resentment."

Gratitude is more than just a fleeting feeling. As brain scans have shown, practicing gratitude can result in lasting changes in the brain, particularly in the prefrontal cortex, heightening our sensitivity to future experiences of gratitude. This reinforces the notion that expressing gratitude during the prayers has long-term positive effects on both spiritual and mental health.

Moreover, gratitude is a concept deeply ingrained in major world religions. Harvard researchers have pointed out that the practice of gratitude benefits not just individuals but society as a whole. As gratitude becomes a trending topic in modern wellness discussions, it is fascinating to note that Islamic prayer, has long embodied gratitude as a fundamental part of worship. From my perspective, Islamic prayer represents the epitome of gratitude, a holistic supplication that balances spiritual, mental, and physical wellness. While other religions also prioritize gratitude in their practices, Islamic prayer offers a unique, deeply immersive form of expression.

My Personal Perspective on Prayer

"What lies behind us and what lies before us are tiny matters compared to what lies within us." –Emerson

Salat is more than a spiritual obligation—it is a discipline that refines the mind, strengthens the will, and cultivates excellence in every aspect of life. Anchoring the day in prayer empowers a person to command their time rather than be consumed by it, structuring life around devotion rather than distraction. Rooted in these sacred pauses, salat instills clarity, consistency, and self-mastery, all essential for success in both spiritual and worldly pursuits. Each prayer becomes a checkpoint, pulling one away from the relentless demands of life to refocus, recalibrate, and renew their connection with the divine.

The rhythm of salat sharpens focus and eliminates procrastination. It trains the body and soul to rise early, act with intention, and cultivate discipline that extends beyond the prayer mat—into work, relationships, and personal growth. In the stillness of Sujud, the burdens of the world dissolve, replaced by resilience and inner peace. The heart finds tranquility in surrender, and the mind, once clouded by chaos, emerges clear and driven.

At its core, salat is also an act of transcendent gratitude—a moment to pause and acknowledge the countless blessings bestowed upon us. With each bow and prostration, the believer humbles themselves before their Creator, expressing thanks not only in words but through disciplined devotion. Gratitude, ingrained within salat, transforms prayer from mere duty into an uplifting force that nurtures contentment, strengthens resilience, and deepens faith. By consistently recognizing divine mercy, the heart remains light, the mind optimistic, and the soul deeply fulfilled.

The decree of five daily prayers is a testament to divine wisdom, a symphony of sacred moments harmonizing devotion with the natural rhythm of life. Like celestial bodies moving in perfect order, these prayers guide the soul through cycles of toil and reflection, action and surrender. Each prayer serves as a guiding beacon, ensuring that no matter how far one drifts into the currents of worldly affairs, they are drawn back to remembrance and purpose. It is neither an excessive burden nor an insufficient measure but the golden mean—a balance that nurtures faith without overwhelming, disciplines the self without breaking, and sanctifies time without disrupting life's flow. These five moments are not interruptions but sanctuaries—divine appointments that illuminate the path, center the heart, and restore the soul to its highest calling.

In a world that constantly pulls people into distractions, salat is an anchor—a force that grounds the believer in purpose, clarity, and unwavering devotion. It is more than a ritual; it is a training of the soul, a means to master the self, conquer the ego, and embody excellence in all aspects of life. Through it, one does not merely pray; one rises, evolves, and embodies the discipline and gratitude needed to achieve both spiritual enlightenment and worldly success.

Like Taoist flow and meditation, these Islamic acts create harmony between the individual and the divine reality, guiding the seeker toward their ultimate purpose: spiritual awakening and closeness to the Creator.

"Prayer is a ladder by which everyone may ascend to heaven." – Rumi

I would like to reflect further and elaborate on my perspectives surrounding prayer and gratitude. I am deeply fond of my prayers and the offerings of gratitude that I give for my life, the people, the experiences, and even the challenges I've encountered along the way. My prayer life has evolved beyond a mere ritual—it has become a deliberate act of aligning my heart, mind, body, and soul to the rhythm of the universe and the will of the

Almighty. When I bow my head in sujud, I feel a cosmic connection to every living thing, every unseen force, and the Creator who governs all.

I make it a point to ensure my prayers are never performed lazily or without intention. There is something sacred in moving through each position—standing, bowing, prostrating, and sitting—with mindfulness and sincerity. I believe that the physical benefits of salat are often overlooked; each motion stretches and realigns the body, improves circulation, and helps center the mind. But beyond the physical, there are powerful mental and spiritual benefits. When I set my intentions with clarity, whether it is to seek forgiveness, express gratitude, or ask for guidance, I notice how these intentions slowly but surely shape my life and my experiences.

This act of prayer serves not only as worship but as an intimate conversation with the divine, where I am reminded of my place in the grand tapestry of existence. And because of this, I strive to make my thoughts, feelings, and intentions deliberate. I aim to align myself with that which is good for me and humanity. When I pray, it's as if I'm setting the course for my soul, and I believe in the power of a well-intentioned prayer to ripple across the universe.

Through the years, I've heard many people—Muslims and non-Muslims alike—criticize the structure of Islamic prayer. Often, it's the same echo, the same undertone dressed in different words:

"Five times a day? That's too much."

"God is with you wherever you go—why do you need formal prayer?"

"God doesn't need you to bow down."

Et cetera, et cetera...

So, let's honestly evaluate these thoughts.

"Five times a day is too much."

Is it? If each prayer takes 10 minutes, that's just 50 minutes out of a 1,440-minute day. That's less than 4% of your time—devoted not to anyone else but to the Source of your breath, your heart, your being. Is that really asking too much? You decide.

"God should be with you wherever you go."

Absolutely—He is. But ask yourself this: if you love someone deeply, don't you still set aside intentional time just for them, even if they're always in your heart? Why would the Divine deserve anything less? You decide.

"God doesn't need you to bow down."

That's true. God is beyond need. But when you bow, it's not for Him— it's for you. The body bends so the soul can rise. The act of lowering yourself humbles the ego, centers the heart, grounds the body, and aligns the spirit. The benefit is entirely yours.

So no—prayer isn't excessive. It's intimate. It's not rigid. It's rhythmic. It's not for God's sake.

It's for yours.

You decide.

As far back as I can remember, I have always possessed a deep sense of gratitude towards life. Whether in moments of joy or sorrow, I have found solace in reflecting on the blessings that have been given to me. Gratitude, in my experience, is not merely an emotion; it is a transformative practice that can shift perspectives and open doors to spiritual insight. Even during the most difficult of times, I have tried to remember the abundance that exists, not just in material wealth, but in the love, wisdom, and experiences that have shaped me.

There have been times in my life, however, when gratitude didn't come easily. I am not exempt from moments of ingratitude or frustration, where the weight of my struggles seemed to overshadow the blessings. In my youth, I felt that asking for more from God was selfish and I should be content with what I had and never desire more. I now realize that this was a limited understanding of the relationship between the Creator and creation. In my maturity, especially after becoming a father, I now feel an obligation to ask for more—not out of greed, but out of trust and hope. The act of asking in itself is an expression of faith, a recognition that God's generosity is boundless.

As a father, I've come to understand this dynamic better. Just as I want my children to feel comfortable asking me for what they need or desire, I believe God wants the same for His creation. It's not about providing everything they ask for without question, but about encouraging them to communicate their needs, to dream, and to trust in the process. Much like I make my children work for the things they ask for, I believe God requires the same from us. I have come to understand that life is a partnership between divine providence and human effort. If I work hard and if it is in my destiny, I trust that God will provide what is best for me, even if it isn't always what I initially wanted.

This lesson became especially poignant during the most difficult time of my life—the tragic loss of my son, Zain. In 2014, my first-born son, who was the gem of my heart, was killed by a reckless driver in my mother's condominium driveway. He was just four years old, and his sudden passing shook my entire existence. I still vividly remember receiving the phone call that something terrible had happened and being told that my son was gone. The drive home that followed felt like an eternity—a two-hour journey filled with unimaginable grief, disbelief, and desperate prayers. I remember pleading with God, bargaining in every way I could: "Please let it be a mistake. Please, just let him be hurt. Let me take his place." I prayed, "Let it be a dream, let it be wrong, let him just be hurt, let him be a vegetable." I prayed and negotiated and made deals that if everything would be ok that I would never do a bad thing again in my life, and I would feed the poor, and I would never miss a prayer, and on and on and on. I made pacts and promises, deals and testaments.

When I finally arrived and saw my son's body covered on the driveway, the reality hit me harder than I could have ever imagined. Despite the overwhelming pain, my very first thought was a prayer of gratitude. I thanked God for the nearly five beautiful years I was blessed to spend with my son. I thanked God for allowing me to experience the boundless love that only a parent can know. I thanked Him for every smile, every laugh, every memory we shared. It was an odd response, but one that has shaped how I have dealt with grief ever since.

In the days, weeks, and months that followed, the sadness was suffocating. There were moments when the darkness threatened to consume me. But slowly, through the fog of grief, I began to remember the joy. I recalled the countless hours I spent with Zain—how our time together was filled with laughter, adventure, and love.

I realized that, by some grace, I had been given an extraordinary amount of time with him. My life circumstances had allowed me to be fully present with my son in ways that many parents aren't afforded. I had a job overseas in Southeast Asia, which paid well. Compounded by the fact that living expenses were also very low, it created a very favorable situation. We traveled together, explored the world, and made memories that I now cherish with all my heart. We had full-time live-in maids and did not have to attend to the daunting, monotonous tasks of keeping the house in order, preparing meals, and other household chores. When we occasionally decided to cook meals together, it was a leisurely, fun activity, and the dishes and clean-up were left to the maids.

We traveled to several countries with my son, and the summers and vacations that we took while in America were second to none. We drove east to west and north to south all over this land, experiencing the densest of forests and the openness of the oceans. We were at the peaks of mountains and at the bases of canyons

Reflecting on these memories brought me a sense of peace, and I understood that my son had lived a full, albeit brief, life. His soul was pure and untouched by the harshness of the world. He was filled with love, curiosity, and kindness. His smile could shatter even the deepest of despair, and I realized that in his short time on Earth, he had experienced more joy and adventure than most people do in a lifetime. And when I considered where he was now—at the side of the Lord—I knew there could be no better place for him.

Gratitude, even in the face of unimaginable loss, became the light that guided me through the darkness and saved me from the depths of despair. It reminded me that, while Zain's physical presence was no longer with me, his essence lives on in the so many grateful memories that I logged during his life and will always carry in my heart.

As I reflect on the lessons of prayer and gratitude, I am reminded that these practices are not just for moments of joy but for times of sorrow as well. They ground us, give us strength, and help us navigate the complexities of life. And so, I continue to pray, to give thanks, and to trust in the wisdom of the divine plan, knowing that everything in this life, both the blessings and the trials, is an opportunity for spiritual growth. That is my story of how gratitude and prayer freed me from the grips of hell.

The scholars unanimously agreed that the fate of children—if they die after the soul has been breathed in and before reaching puberty—is Paradise, as an honor from Allah, may He be exalted, to them and their parents, and as a mercy from Him, Whose mercy encompasses all things.

"Inna lillahi wa inna ilayhi raji'un"
(Indeed, to Allah we belong and to Allah we shall return.)
Surah Baqarah ayat 156:

"The wound is the place where the light enters you."
–Rumi

Rest in peace
Zain Hussain
5th July 2009–11th April 2014

"When you are sorrowful, look again in your heart, and you shall see that in truth you are weeping for that which has been your delight." –Kahlil Gibran

ZAKAT (CHARITY)

"I slept and I dreamed that life is all joy. I woke, and I saw that life is all service. I served, and I saw that service is joy."
−Kahlil Gibran

Zakat (zah-kaat) is an Arabic term that refers to the obligatory almsgiving or charity tax in Islamic tradition. Among the Five Pillars of Islam, zakat stands out as a form of worship that is both personal and communal. It transcends the individual, uplifting the entire society. Zakat is not simply about giving; it is about purification. It is derived from the root word "zaka," which means to purify or cleanse, signifying the cleansing of one's wealth and soul through charity. In Islam, zakat is not viewed as an optional act of kindness but as a divine commandment and a crucial moral responsibility. In both Islam and Taoism, the act of giving is not merely a transaction but a circulation of energy, a sacred exchange that aligns individuals with the greater harmony of existence. Just as water must flow to remain pure, wealth and resources must move freely to maintain balance, avoiding stagnation and the corruption of excess.

In Taoism, the principle of Shu (reciprocity and mutual benefit) emphasizes the natural exchange of giving and receiving. Taoist masters often teach that hoarding energy—whether material wealth, emotions, or knowledge—creates imbalance. By circulating resources, whether tangible or intangible, one aligns with the Tao (The Way), ensuring harmony and prosperity.

"The sage does not hoard. The more he helps others, the more he benefits. The more he gives to others, the more he possesses." (Tao Te Ching 81)

Zakat is one of the most powerful, positive, and beneficial pillars in Islam. It requires Muslims who meet specific financial criteria to contribute 2.5% of their eligible annual wealth to charity. This is calculated based on cash, business assets, gold, silver, agricultural produce, and livestock. It serves as a means of balancing wealth, assisting the less fortunate, and reducing the gap between the rich and poor. By redistributing wealth, zakat plays a pivotal role in promoting social justice and harmony in society.

As a Muslim, if your wealth exceeds a certain amount, called *nisab*, "nee-saab" you are required to pay zakat. The wealth subject to zakat is carefully calculated, ensuring that it's given in the proper proportion, with the correct intention, and distributed to the eligible recipients. These recipients are categorized in the Quran and include the poor, the needy, those in debt, individuals striving in the way of Islam, and those seeking to free themselves from bondage or slavery.

Zakat holds profound spiritual significance. It is more than a financial transaction; it is an act of spiritual growth and moral elevation. By giving a portion of one's wealth, an individual becomes more connected with humanity, possessing empathy and solidarity with the underprivileged. This act of selflessness is a way to harmonize oneself with the natural flow of the universe. In the cosmic order of things, everything has been created in balance, and charity is a means by which we align ourselves with that balance, fulfilling our duty to care for one another.

Moreover, zakat carries immense personal benefits. Charity isn't just for the benefit of the receiver—it transforms the giver. For many, parting with hard-earned money can be difficult, and this struggle is part of the purification process. It detaches us from the material world and reminds us that wealth is not solely for personal enjoyment but is a trust from Allah. Those who are not in a financial position to give can still participate in acts of charity by offering their time and services, which can be just as rewarding and beneficial.

Psychological research shows that giving and serving others can lead to a multitude of mental and physical health benefits. One study suggests that spending money on others positively impacts cardiovascular health, thereby offering a pathway by which pro-social behavior improves physical health among at-risk adults. When we give with an open heart, our brain releases "feel-good" chemicals, such as serotonin, dopamine, and oxytocin. These chemicals lower blood pressure, reduce cortisol levels (the stress hormone), and combat feelings of anxiety and depression. This connection between giving and health underscores how closely our emotional well-being is tied to acts of charity. (Whillans et al., 2016)

As neuroscientist Andrew Huberman reviewed in his research on gratitude and generosity, receiving gratitude is one of the most powerful forms of emotional experience for the human brain. As Huberman says, "Turns out that the most potent form of gratitude practices not a gratitude practice where you are expressing gratitude but rather where you receive gratitude, where you receive thanks. Receiving gratitude is much more potent in terms of the positive shifts that they can create than giving gratitude."

I feel that this exchange of energy, where the giver feels appreciation from the receiver, resonates at a high frequency that amplifies positivity in the heart and mind of the giver. It is as if the vulnerability of the one receiving charity is mirrored back to the giver, magnified tenfold, in a cosmic act of karmic retribution. Receiving gratitude enhances our sense of worth and solidifies the bonds of community. Through giving, we cultivate a deep connection to the world and nurture an inner peace that extends far beyond material possessions.

Beyond the immediate benefits of giving, zakat has the potential to leave an enduring social impact. When practiced collectively, zakat becomes a tool for uplifting entire communities. It can fund initiatives that address long-term solutions to poverty, such as education, healthcare, housing, and employment opportunities. When distributed effectively, zakat strengthens the fabric of society, fostering cohesion and reducing social inequality. In a world where disparity often breeds conflict, zakat serves as a reminder of our shared humanity and the obligation to care for those less fortunate.

This principle of selfless service can be summed up by the words of Denzel Washington: "The most selfish thing you can do in this world is helping someone else because the gratification, the goodness that comes to you, the good feeling, the good feeling from helping others—nothing is better than that. Not jewelry, not the big house, not the cars; it's the joy."

Zakat is not just an economic obligation; it is a sacred duty to uplift others and maintain the well-being of the community. Taoism likewise teaches that when one contributes to the balance of the collective, they are also aligning themselves with the flow of divine abundance.

To give is to trust—trust in the divine order and in God's infinite provision. Through charity, we remove fear, cultivate generosity, and affirm our faith in a universe that operates through cycles of giving and receiving.

Both Islam and Taoism teach that giving is not loss—it is alignment. When we give without hesitation, we move closer to the divine, closer to balance, and closer to true prosperity.

Similarly, Mahatma Gandhi once said: "The best way to find yourself is to lose yourself in the service of others."

This philosophy mirrors the essence of zakat and charity in Islam: through selflessness, we transcend the material world and find deeper meaning and fulfillment.

In conclusion, zakat is not merely a financial obligation—it is a spiritual practice that purifies the heart and uplifts the soul. It reminds us of our responsibility to our fellow human beings and allows us to cultivate a life of service, humility, and gratitude. Through zakat, we are given the opportunity to not only help those in need but to strengthen our own faith, deepen our compassion, and create a more just and equitable world. When we serve others, we embody a sense of unity and create a ripple effect of positivity that transcends borders, cultures, and religions.

Prophet Muhammad taught that "the best of people are those who are most beneficial to others." –Hadith, Al-Mu'jam al-Awsaṭ

The Bloom of Benevolence

Charity, like a delicate bloom gracing the earth, possesses the power to nurture and uplift the world in myriad ways. It is a luminous thread woven through the fabric of human existence, connecting hearts and fostering compassion. Through acts of selflessness and giving, charity radiates a profound impact, like a sunlit garden blooming with beauty. Its petals unfold in the form of shelter for the homeless, sustenance for the hungry, education for the marginalized, and solace for the afflicted. As each gesture of kindness takes flight, it ripples across the tapestry of humanity, nurturing hope, fostering resilience, and igniting a spark of transformation. In the embrace of charity, the world is infused with a radiant warmth, a tender reminder that we are all interconnected, that our shared humanity calls us to reach out, to uplift one another. For when we extend a helping hand, we not only alleviate suffering but also sow the seeds of empowerment and renewal. Charity is the fragrance that permeates the air, inspiring generosity, and awakening the noblest aspirations within us. It reminds us that in the act of giving, we find purpose and fulfillment, for it is in selflessly serving others that we discover our own true essence. So let us cultivate this garden of charity, tending to its blossoms with unwavering devotion, and witness as its resplendent beauty illuminates the world with boundless love and compassion.

–Ah Lee

SAWM (FASTING)

Ramadan is a time of discipline, self-reflection, and spiritual growth. Training during this holy month requires additional dedication and sacrifice, but it strengthens not only the body but also the soul.
–Khabib Nurmagomedov

For centuries, fasting has been recognized as a powerful tool for both spiritual refinement and physical renewal. In Islam, fasting, or *sawm*, is not merely a temporary abstinence from physical indulgences but a transformative spiritual discipline deeply embedded in the Islamic tradition. It carries the weight of sacred intention, connecting believers to the divine and offering them a chance to step beyond their everyday routines into a realm of purification, reflection, and transformation. Fasting is not just a physical act; it is an intimate journey that engages the mind, body, and soul, allowing believers to cultivate a deeper connection with God while experiencing numerous health benefits. Taoist philosophy embraces the idea of periodic fasting as a means of harmonizing the body's natural energies, expelling toxins, and realigning with the Tao—the fundamental flow of existence.

During the month of Ramadan, Muslims around the world embark on a sacred journey, fasting from dawn to sunset and abstaining from food, drink, smoking, and intimate relations. This period is not only about physical restraint but also a time for believers to engage in self-discipline and spiritual growth. Ramadan is celebrated as the month in which the Quran was revealed to Prophet Muhammad (PBUH), offering guidance and clarity to humanity. The Quran reminds us, "The month of Ramadan is that in which was revealed the Quran, a guidance for the people and clear proofs of guidance and criterion. So whoever sights the new moon of the month, let him fast it" (Quran 2:185).

Islam's reliance on a lunar calendar means that Ramadan shifts through the seasons over the years, offering believers a chance to experience fasting under varying conditions. As a result, the fast is sometimes tested by the long, hot days of summer and, at other times, the shorter, cooler days of winter. This cyclical nature teaches adaptability and serves as a reminder of the ever-changing nature of life itself. Regardless of the season, the essence of fasting remains constant—an invitation to look beyond the physical world and reconnect with the eternal.

The practice of fasting in Islam is both a call to discipline and a testament to God's mercy. While fasting during Ramadan is a pillar of Islam, there is a recognition that not everyone can partake in this rigorous practice. Those with chronic illnesses, pregnant or nursing mothers, menstruating women, young children, and the elderly are exempted, as their well-being is prioritized over the physical act of fasting. Travelers who cover more than fifty miles and those engaged in arduous tasks may also delay their fast until a more suitable time.

Yet, the compassionate nature of these exemptions does not negate the spiritual commitment. Believers who miss fasts for temporary reasons are required to make up the missed days after Ramadan and before the next year's fast. For those who are permanently unable to fast, *fidya*— "fid-yah" feeding a needy person for each missed day—is prescribed. This balance between obligation and mercy underscores the inclusiveness of fasting in Islam. It serves as a reminder that the ultimate goal of fasting is not mere physical deprivation but the purification of the heart and soul.

Fasting each day begins with the pre-dawn meal known as suhoor (soo-hoor). This meal, consumed before the *fajr* prayer, is a source of blessing and strength throughout the day. The Prophet Muhammad (PBUH) emphasized the importance of suhoor, saying, "Eat suhoor, for in suhoor there is blessing." (Sahih Bukhari 1923, Sahih Muslim 1095) It is a time of quiet reflection, where the believer nourishes the body before the day's spiritual endeavor.

As the sun sets, the day-long fast is broken with *iftar* (if-tar), a meal that symbolizes both gratitude and humility. Traditionally, Muslims break their fast with dates and water, emulating the simplicity of the Prophet's practice. Dates provide a quick source of energy, offering a moment of sweetness after a day of restraint. Yet, in modern times, iftar has become a moment of overindulgence for many, turning into a feast that contrasts sharply with the day's fasting. Lavish spreads and elaborate dishes have become common, leading to an excess that contradicts the very spirit of restraint and reflection that Ramadan embodies. The Prophet's guidance was clear: "The son of Adam does not fill any vessel worse than his stomach. It is sufficient for the son of Adam to eat a few mouthfuls, to keep him going..." (al-Tirmidhi) 2380.

This tendency to indulge at iftar not only undermines the physical benefits of fasting but also distracts from its spiritual purpose. The fast is meant to cultivate a sense of gratitude, mindfulness, and empathy for those who endure hunger daily—not to be undone by the excesses of a single meal. True fasting requires that the restraint of the day extend into the evening and that the discipline of the soul carries over into the heart's desires. It is a reminder that one should not only refrain from physical indulgences but also from wicked thoughts and deeds. As the Prophet Muhammad (PBUH) said, "Whoever does not give up false statements and evil deeds while fasting, then Allah is not in need of his leaving his food and drink" (Jami' at-Tirmidhi 2380, Sunan Ibn Majah 3349).

Fasting is a crucible in which the spirit is refined and the ego is subdued. By abstaining from food, drink, and other physical desires, believers are reminded of their capacity for control over the self. This process is not about punishment but about training the heart to resist the temptations that often cloud our judgment. It is a reminder that the true battle lies within—against one's own inclinations toward excess, impatience, and distraction.

This discipline is not limited to the physical domain; it extends to the mental and emotional realms. Believers are called to exercise patience, to speak with kindness, and to refrain from anger and negativity. The practice of fasting is a daily exercise in self-restraint that continues long after the sunset meal. It instills virtues that transcend the boundaries of Ramadan, possessing a resilience that benefits all aspects of life.

Furthermore, fasting nurtures a transformative sense of empathy. When one voluntarily experiences hunger, even for a day, the plight of those who suffer from food insecurity year-round becomes more tangible. This awareness drives Muslims to engage in acts of charity during Ramadan, such as zakat or sadaqah (sad-ah-kah), which means voluntary giving. Fasting, therefore, is not merely a solitary act of devotion but a means of bridging the gap between the self and the collective, between individual devotion and societal responsibility.

The benefits of fasting extend beyond spiritual growth; they offer a much-needed respite for the body, particularly the digestive system. Under normal circumstances, digestion is an intricate process involving the breakdown of food into smaller components. Enzymes and acids work to digest proteins, carbohydrates, and fats, transforming them into nutrients that are absorbed through the stomach and intestines. This process is energy-intensive, diverting significant bodily resources toward breaking down and assimilating food.

When the body is engaged in constant digestion, there is little opportunity for other processes, such as cellular repair, to occur. Fasting, however, provides a temporary pause from this demanding activity, allowing the body to focus on healing and rejuvenation. During this time, the body can shift its attention to processes like autophagy, where cells break down damaged components and recycle them into new, healthy cells (*Nature*, 2016). This rest for the digestive system allows it to regain balance and efficiency, much like a machine that requires occasional downtime to function optimally. The relief brought about by fasting allows the body to renew itself, highlighting the wisdom in this ancient practice.

One of the most amazing physical benefits of fasting is autophagy, a natural process that allows the body to clean out damaged cells and regenerate new ones. The term "autophagy" comes from the Greek "auto" meaning self, and "phagy" meaning eating—essentially meaning "self-eating." During fasting, the body initiates this self-cleansing process, forming autophagosomes around damaged proteins and organelles. These autophagosomes merge with lysosomes, breaking down the contents into reusable components (*Nature*, 2016). Autophagy plays a critical role in maintaining cellular health, reducing inflammation, and preventing diseases such as cancer and neurodegenerative disorders (*Nature*, 2016).

Dr. Luiza Petre, a board-certified cardiologist, describes autophagy as "recycling and cleaning at the same time, just like hitting a reset button to your body." This mechanism not only promotes cellular repair but also extends the lifespan of cells, supporting overall longevity. Priya Khorana, Ph.D., explains that autophagy is an adaptive mechanism that allows the body to survive and thrive during periods of stress and nutrient scarcity. Fasting, therefore, is more than a physical act—it is a biological reset, allowing the body to rejuvenate and maintain optimal health.

Fasting is a practice that transcends the boundaries of Islam, reflecting a universal human yearning for spiritual elevation through physical restraint. In Christianity, fasting is mentioned frequently in the Bible, with Jesus himself said to have fasted for forty days and forty nights. This period of fasting, known as Lent, is a time of repentance, reflection, and spiritual renewal. Jesus taught his followers, "When you fast, do not look somber as the hypocrites do... But when you fast, put oil on your head and wash your face" (Matthew 6:16–17), emphasizing that fasting is a private and sincere act of devotion to God.

In Taoist thought, the concept of "internal cleansing" is a fundamental aspect of longevity practices. Taoist sages advocated for periods of food abstinence to purge stagnant Qi (energy) and revitalize the body's internal organs. They believed that excessive eating burdens the digestive system, leading to disease and imbalance. Fasting, therefore, was seen as a method of realigning the body's natural flow of energy with the cosmic order.

In Judaism, fasting is observed on Yom Kippur, the Day of Atonement, as a means of seeking forgiveness and spiritual cleansing. It is a time when believers refrain from eating, drinking, and other physical pleasures, focusing instead on prayer and repentance. This mirrors the themes of self-purification and humility found in Islamic fasting, where the goal is to realign the soul with the divine.

Hinduism and Buddhism also embrace fasting as a path to spiritual clarity. Hindu practitioners fast on specific days, such as Ekadashi, to seek blessings and deepen their devotion. In Buddhism, fasting is used to cultivate mindfulness and to control desires, often accompanying meditation to attain deeper spiritual insights. In all traditions, fasting is seen not merely as an act of abstinence but as a transformative process that purifies the mind and heart.

These diverse practices demonstrate that fasting is a shared tradition across humanity, a universal response to the call for spiritual growth. Each tradition, while unique in its practices, echoes a common truth: that through the voluntary surrender of physical comforts, the soul can draw closer to the eternal.

The Health Benefits of Fasting

Fasting offers numerous scientifically verified health benefits, extending beyond its spiritual dimensions. Below is a list of some of the most significant benefits supported by research:

- **Promotes Blood Sugar Control and Reduces Insulin Resistance**: Improves insulin sensitivity, making it especially beneficial for individuals with type 2 diabetes (*Diabetologia*, 2014).

- **Enhances Weight Loss and Boosts Metabolism**: Increases metabolism through elevated production of norepinephrine, facilitating fat loss (*American Journal of Clinical Nutrition*, 2016).

- **Activates Autophagy for Cellular Repair**: Removes damaged cells, allowing for cellular regeneration and potentially reducing the risk of cancer (*Nature*, 2016).

- **Reduces Inflammation**: Decreases markers like C-reactive protein (CRP) and interleukin-6 (IL-6), helping to combat chronic inflammation (*Nutrients*, 2019).

- **Improves Heart Health**: Lowers blood pressure, reduces LDL cholesterol, and enhances overall cardiovascular function (*Hypertension*, 2018).

- **Boosts Brain Function**: Increases brain-derived neurotrophic factor (BDNF) levels, promoting cognitive function and protecting against neurodegenerative diseases (*Neurobiology of Disease*, 2018).

- **Supports Longevity**: Extends lifespan and slows aging by reducing oxidative stress and promoting cellular health (*Cell Metabolism*, 2017).

- **Facilitates Liver Detoxification**: Stimulates liver function, enhancing the body's ability to eliminate toxins (*Hepatology*, 2015).

- **Improves Digestive System Health**: Allows the digestive system to rest, improving nutrient absorption and gut microbiome balance (*Journal of Gastroenterology*, 2018).

- **Increases Human Growth Hormone (HGH) Production**: Boosts HGH levels, aiding in muscle strength, metabolism, and overall growth (*The Journal of Clinical Endocrinology & Metabolism*, 2001).

- **Enhances Immune System Functioning**: Promotes the regeneration of white blood cells, improving immune response (*Cell Stem Cell*, 2014).

- **May Aid in Cancer Prevention**: Slows the growth of cancer cells and increases their sensitivity to treatment (*Cancer Cell*, 2015).

- **Improves Sleep Quality**: Stabilizes blood sugar levels, leading to improved sleep efficiency and reduced nighttime awakenings (*Journal of Sleep Research*, 2018).
- **Promotes Ketosis for Fat Burning**: Shifts the body's metabolism to burning fat for fuel, which is useful for weight loss (*Frontiers in Physiology*, 2018).
- **Enhances Athletic Performance**: Optimizes fat usage during exercise, improving endurance in athletes (*Journal of the International Society of Sports Nutrition*, 2016).
- **Fasting during Ramadan on RA activity**: The findings suggested that such fasting led to a rapid improvement in rheumatoid arthritis symptoms, with positive effects lasting up to three months post-fasting.("Sustainable positive effects of Ramadan intermittent fasting in rheumatoid arthritis." Clinical rheumatology vol. 41,2 (2022).

Fasting creates a unique opportunity for the soul to grow, the mind to reflect, and the heart to connect with the divine. The soul, through fasting, is invited into the space of *dhikr*, "dh-ikr" remembrance of God, and in this sacred remembrance, the soul finds its true nourishment. In the silence of hunger and in the simplicity of abstinence, the believer draws nearer to the divine presence, breaking through the veils that obscure the heart from its Lord. This spiritual stillness allows the believer to experience the profound connection between body and soul, moving beyond the material realm to seek proximity to God.

Fasting in Islam is a sacred invitation to step beyond the material world and connect deeply with the divine. It is a pathway to transformation, guiding believers toward self-discovery, discipline, and spiritual awakening. Through the challenges of hunger and restraint, fasting teaches us that true sustenance is not found in material consumption but in the nourishment of the soul through remembrance of God. The dual nature of fasting—its physical and spiritual dimensions—highlights the holistic nature of Islamic teachings, where spiritual and physical well-being are deeply intertwined.

The scientifically backed benefits of fasting, from promoting cellular repair and reducing inflammation to supporting mental clarity and metabolic health, underscore the wisdom of fasting as a practice that nurtures the mind, body, and spirit. As the believer fasts, they learn that strength lies not in the satisfaction of desires but in the ability to rise above them, to seek closeness to the Creator. Fasting is a sacred gift, a means of aligning the soul with its divine purpose and emerging from the month of Ramadan transformed, renewed, and ready to continue the journey toward spiritual excellence. In the modern world—where overconsumption is the norm—fasting reminds us that sometimes, **less is more.**

"Fasting blinds the body in order to open the eyes of the soul."
–Rumi

HAJJ (PILGRIMAGE)

"The Hajj is a transformative experience. It challenges the ego, the status, the privileges, and forces the pilgrim to see himself as nothing more than a servant of God." –Karen Armstrong

Across cultures and faiths, the act of pilgrimage represents a journey of the soul, a sacred undertaking that transcends the physical realm and serves as a passage toward spiritual awakening, renewal, and deeper connection with the divine. Hajj, the annual pilgrimage to the holy city of Mecca in Saudi Arabia, stands as one of the five foundational pillars of Islam. It is a fundamental journey of faith, unity, and submission to God, a religious duty incumbent upon every able-bodied Muslim who can afford it. More than a physical journey, hajj is a sacred experience that transforms the soul, reconnects the believer with their Creator, and fosters a sense of unity and humility among Muslims from diverse backgrounds. It is a time of reflection, seeking forgiveness, and building a stronger connection with Allah, as well as with the global Muslim community.

Whether in Taoism, Buddhism, Christianity, Hinduism, or indigenous traditions, sacred journeys serve a similar function: they are tests of faith, endurance, and devotion, where the traveler is refined through the very act of movement. Taoism, deeply rooted in the natural order of existence, does not emphasize a single holy site for pilgrimage in the way that Islam or Christianity might. Instead, sacred mountains, temples, and mystical caves serve as places of retreat and transformation. Buddhist pilgrimage is deeply contemplative, often requiring long, arduous journeys to detach from the material world and cultivate mindfulness, simplicity, and spiritual awakening. Like hajj, these journeys symbolize leaving behind attachments and stepping into a higher state of consciousness.

Pilgrimage in Christianity is seen as a journey of devotion, penance, and reflection. Christians seek to walk in the footsteps of Jesus (PBUH) and the saints, visiting sites of biblical and historical significance, like Jerusalem, the most sacred city for Christians, home to the Church of the Holy Sepulchre, the site of Jesus' crucifixion and resurrection.

Christian pilgrimage often involves prayer, fasting, and acts of devotion, embodying a spiritual journey that mirrors the trials and tribulations of faith itself.

Hajj encompasses a series of rituals that commemorate the actions of the Prophet Ibrahim (Abraham), his wife Hagar, and their son Ishmael. Each ritual holds profound spiritual significance and serves as a reminder of unwavering faith, sacrifice, and God's mercy. The pilgrimage begins with the *ihram*, which is a state of purity and consecration. Ihram represents the shedding of worldly attachments and prepares the pilgrim to focus solely on their Creator. Pilgrims don simple white garments, which symbolize equality and unity, stripping away any markers of social status, wealth, or nationality.

The next ritual of hajj includes *tawaf*, the act of circumambulating the Kaaba, the sacred cube-shaped structure at the heart of the Grand Mosque. Moving in a counterclockwise direction around the Kaaba, millions of pilgrims express their devotion and humility to God, joining in a flow that mirrors the movement of the universe itself.

Pilgrims then perform *sa'i*, which involves walking and running between the hills of Safa and Marwa, retracing the steps of Hagar as she searched for water for her son Ishmael. This act is a testament to perseverance and divine providence, reminding the believer that God's aid comes to those who strive with sincerity.

The pilgrimage reaches its spiritual zenith on the plain of Arafat, where pilgrims gather to engage in supplication, self-reflection, and seeking forgiveness. Known as the Day of Arafat, it is a time when the boundaries between the earthly and the divine seem to dissolve, and the believer's heart is laid bare before God. This day is a profound reminder of the Day of Judgment, where every soul will stand alone before their Creator.

After sunset, pilgrims proceed to Muzdalifah, spending the night under the open sky, gathering pebbles to use in the symbolic stoning of the devil at Mina. This act represents the rejection of evil and the commitment to resisting temptation.

The journey continues with an animal sacrifice, echoing the story of Abraham's willingness to sacrifice his son in obedience to God. Pilgrims offer a sheep or goat, sharing the meat with the needy as an expression of gratitude and devotion. This act embodies the spirit of sacrifice and charity that is central to hajj. Pilgrims then return to Mecca to perform another tawaf and sa'i, followed by the farewell tawaf, bidding farewell to the Kaaba with hearts full of gratitude and awe.

Dr. Jordan Peterson, a renowned psychologist, articulates the transformative power of pilgrimage, emphasizing that it is far more than a physical journey. "The act of embarking on a physical journey to a sacred or significant place can have profound psychological and spiritual effects on an individual." He suggests that stepping out of one's familiar surroundings and venturing into the unknown serves as a form of symbolic rebirth—a detachment from the routines and constraints of daily life that allows for deeper introspection and renewal. This resonates deeply with the experience of hajj, where millions leave behind their homes, communities, and comforts to immerse themselves in a journey that demands physical effort, spiritual openness, and a willingness to confront one's limitations.

For Peterson, the significance of pilgrimage lies in the symbolic and metaphorical aspects of the journey. It is a voluntary confrontation with the self—a chance to face fears, acknowledge limitations, and seek a deeper understanding of life's meaning. Pilgrims engage in a process of self-reflection, confronting the depths of their own hearts amidst the vastness of the desert and the majesty of the Kaaba. In doing so, they experience a transformation that is both personal and enlightening. This echoes the words of the Prophet Muhammad (PBUH), who emphasized the purifying nature of hajj, saying, "Whoever performs Hajj for the sake of Allah, avoiding obscene speech and sinful behavior, will return as pure as the day they were born" (Bukhari).

The essence of hajj lies not only in individual transformation but also in the powerful sense of unity and equality it fosters. El-Hajj Malik El-Shabazz, more widely known as Malcolm X, captured this sentiment during his pilgrimage to Mecca in 1964 when racial tensions in America were nearly at a peak between black and white Americans. In a letter from Mecca, he wrote:

"Never have I witnessed such sincere hospitality and overwhelming spirit of true brotherhood as is practiced by people of all colors and races here in this ancient holy land, the home of Abraham, Prophet Muhammad (PBUH), and all the other Prophets of the Holy Scriptures ... For the past week, I have been utterly speechless and spellbound by the graciousness I see displayed all around me by people of all colors. There were tens of thousands of pilgrims from all over the world. They were of all colors, from blue-eyed blonds to black-skinned Africans. But we were all participating in the same ritual, displaying a spirit of unity and brotherhood that my experiences in America had led me to believe never could exist between the white and non-white."

Malcolm X's experience in Mecca during hajj was life-altering and led him to abandon his earlier ideology of racial separatism and embrace a more inclusive vision of humanity. Witnessing people of different races, ethnicities, and backgrounds united in worship and devotion to one God reshaped his perspective. He saw that the Oneness of God could lead to a true oneness of humanity, a vision that stood in stark contrast to the systemic racism he had encountered in America. His words reflect a realization that the teachings of Islam offered a powerful remedy to the divisions and inequalities that plagued his homeland.

Hajj demands a deep sense of surrender, echoing the submission of Abraham and his family. The pilgrimage asks each believer to sacrifice comfort, endure physical hardships, and surrender to the will of God. It is a journey that tests physical strength and spiritual fortitude, challenging pilgrims to maintain their intention and focus amidst the intensity of the experience. Yet, it is in this surrender that pilgrims find their true strength. As Dr. Peterson notes, the act of pilgrimage compels individuals to, "Connect with something larger than themselves," allowing them to tap into a sense of awe, reverence, and humility.

This sense of surrender is vividly expressed in the simple white garments of *ihram*, which strip away worldly distinctions and remind each pilgrim that they stand before God as equals. In the sea of white, there is no rich or poor, no king or servant—only believers united in their devotion. This profound equality allows for a collective experience of humility and gratitude, a shared acknowledgment that all are dependent on the mercy of God.

The physical rigor of hajj serves as a reminder of the discipline required in spiritual life. Pilgrims walk great distances, endure the heat of the desert, and engage in physically demanding rituals, all while maintaining a state of spiritual focus. This discipline mirrors the broader teachings of Islam, which encourage believers to cultivate self-control and resilience. The ability to endure hardship and sacrifice comfort for the sake of a higher purpose is a key lesson that pilgrims take back to their daily lives. Pilgrims are called to refrain not only from physical indulgences but also from negative thoughts, harsh speech, and sinful behavior. The pilgrimage thus becomes a holistic exercise in self-restraint, where the outer journey mirrors the inner journey of the heart.

Hajj, like all true pilgrimages, is a journey that transcends the physical realm. It is an opportunity to leave behind the familiar and immerse oneself in the divine presence. As Malcolm X described, the experience of standing on the plain of Arafat, surrounded by believers of every color and background, was a powerful testament to the unity of humanity. This unity, born of a shared submission to the Creator, reflects the deeper truth of hajj—that it is not only a physical journey but a metaphysical one, where the believer encounters the reality of God's mercy and majesty.

Pilgrims return from hajj with hearts transformed, their souls having been refined in the crucible of devotion. They carry with them a renewed sense of purpose, a deeper understanding of their place in the universe, and a commitment to living in accordance with the teachings of Islam. This transformation is not a fleeting moment but a profound shift that shapes the believer's life long after the pilgrimage is over.

Hajj is a divine gift, a call to step beyond the ordinary and into the realm of the sacred. It is a journey that invites the believer to surrender to God, to embrace humility, and to experience the transformative power of unity and devotion. Through physical hardships and spiritual challenges, hajj teaches that true strength lies in surrender and that the deepest fulfillment is found in submission to God's will.

The words of Dr. Jordan Peterson and Malcolm X echo the enduring truths of hajj: that it is a journey of self-discovery, a confrontation with one's limitations, and a path to a deeper connection with the Creator. As Malcolm X reflected, *"All praise is due to Allah, the Lord of all the Worlds."* Hajj is not merely a pilgrimage to a distant land; it is a journey inward, where the believer's heart becomes a sanctuary for the divine presence. It is a journey that transcends time and space, leading each pilgrim toward a renewed sense of purpose, a deeper understanding of their faith, and a life forever changed by the experience of standing before the Kaaba, the house of God.

HALAL AND HARAM

A Sacred Balance of Life and Ethical Integrity

Your mind must be stronger than your feelings.
–Andrew Tate

HALAL

"We are what we repeatedly do. Excellence, then is not an act, but a habit."
(Durant 1926 on Aristotle)

Halal is often understood primarily in the context of how an animal is slaughtered to prepare it for consumption. However, this view simplifies an intricate symbiotic principle of practice. Halal embodies a benevolent approach to ethical treatment, ensuring that every step—from the animal's life to its slaughter—is carried out with compassion, dignity, and respect. It emphasizes the importance of humane handling, proper care, and adherence to spiritual principles. The act of slaughter itself is just one part of a broader framework that aligns with values of purity, responsibility, and gratitude, making the consumption of food an act of spiritual significance rather than a mere physical necessity.

In Islam, the concepts of *halal* (permissible) and *haram* (forbidden) are not just rules but reflections of the divine order, a reminder of the sacred balance between life, consumption, and spiritual well-being. Living according to these principles transforms the mundane into the sacred, where every action, from eating to speaking, becomes an opportunity to align oneself with the will of our compassionate Creator. They represent the embodiment of a deeper truth: that we are caretakers of this Earth, charged with the responsibility of protecting the purity and sanctity of all life, human and non-human alike. Similarly, the Jewish faith prescribes Jews to eat Kosher. Though halal and kosher systems have differences in their rules and traditions, both reflect a sacred sense of gratitude, discipline, and compassion toward food consumption. These dietary laws encourage mindfulness, community cohesion, and ethical eating in ways that transcend their religious boundaries. In today's world, their principles inspire people of all backgrounds to think critically about sustainability, ethics, and the spiritual significance of food.

These are the main conditions that must be met for an animal to be considered legitimately halal to eat:

- The animal must be treated with dignity and respect prior to the slaughter. Meaning the animal must have lived its life in a good environment and condition, preferably without scars or injury.
- The feeding of animal by-products is prohibited.
- Animals must have access to drinking water until they are slaughtered.
- Slaughter must be accomplished by any Muslim who has reached puberty or Jews and Christian (People of the Book). The person should have knowledge of the proper halal method.
- The reference to God must be pronounced before or as the animal is being slaughtered.
- The animal's face should be pointed towards Mecca.
- The knife must be very sharp and the edge of the blade perfectly smooth (no nicks in the blade).
- The knife must not be sharpened in the presence of animals to be slaughtered (to avoid potential undue stress on the animal).
- The halal process involves one pass of the blade across the throat of the animal, severing the carotid arteries, jugular vein, and trachea.
- The age of the animal is a consideration in Halal requirements. Generally, the animal must be of a mature age at the time of slaughter. The exact definition of maturity may vary depending on the animal species.
- The animals must be allowed to bleed out completely.

- Animals should not be witness to the slaughter of other animals.

Halal represents a cognizant way of living, grounded in purity, righteousness, and ethical conduct. It emphasizes and embodies a comprehensive and conscious pursuit of what is wholesome and beneficial (tayyib) while avoiding what is harmful or impure. This framework reflects a deep commitment and encourages individuals to align every aspect of their lives—whether through behavior, business practices, or interpersonal interactions—with moral and spiritual principles. Living halal nurtures not just the body but also the soul, creating a mindful lifestyle centered on gratitude, compassion, and integrity, ensuring that one's lifestyle promotes well-being for oneself, the community, and the environment

Living *halal* means choosing a life of integrity guided by compassion, mindfulness, and ethical awareness. Every action becomes a form of worship, from the way we treat others to how we respect the world around us. By eating *halal*, we are not only following dietary laws but also safeguarding our spiritual purity. The food we consume becomes a reflection of our inner state, and this connection between the material and the spiritual is central to living in harmony with God's will.

This divine command to consume what is pure extends beyond mere nourishment. It calls us to engage with the world in a way that imparts justice and kindness. The Prophet Muhammad (PBUH) taught that "A body nourished with *haram* will not enter Paradise" (Tirmidhi), a stark reminder that what we put into our bodies shapes the condition of our souls. To live *halal* is to honor this profound relationship between body and spirit, ensuring that every bite, every action, reflects the divine light of God's guidance.

HARAM

"Knowing is not enough; we must apply. Willing is not enough; we must do."
–Bruce Lee

Conversely, *haram* represents what pollutes the soul, harms the body, and disrupts this sacred balance, severing the connection between body, mind, and spirit.

It is the darkness that pulls us away from our divine purpose, encouraging mindless indulgence and disconnection from God. Haram encompasses more than just what is unlawful—it reflects what separates the soul from divine alignment, tainting both spirit and society. Activities such as associating partners with God (shirk), engaging in witchcraft, usury, backbiting, slander, adultery, intoxication, and fornication are not merely prohibited but represent spiritual poisons. Each haram act draws the soul away from the remembrance of the divine, disrupting the harmony from within.

These actions strike at the very foundation of our energy, motivation, and discipline, the divine tools we have been entrusted with to fulfill our purpose on Earth. I believe we are facing a spiritual assault on an existential level of existence as if a veil of heedlessness has fallen over us. Consuming conventional meats, laden with toxins and devoid of barakah (blessings), drains us of vitality, while intoxicants cloud the mind, blocking the heart's connection with our Source power. These pollutants act as chains, binding us to a lower state of being, where apathy and sluggishness take the place of spiritual striving.

Modern distractions such as intoxicants, pornography, television, and endless streaming services numb the soul. They lower our vibrational state to that of automatons detached from the sacred pulse of life. I believe that beneath the surface of this entertainment lies a more insidious agenda, one that subtly shapes the mind to accept immoral and demonic influences. This agenda, if one follows thought through to conclusion, surely the destination one will arrive at hedonism. From songs that glorify vice to videos depicting idols basking in hellish imagery, the soul is bombarded with messages that normalize sin and alienate us from God. Never before has humanity been so bombarded with distractions. The modern age is one of constant notifications, social media scrolling, and an unending cycle of entertainment. The ability to sit in stillness, to reflect deeply, or to connect with the divine is often sacrificed at the altar of endless digital engagement. Instead of using technology as a tool for growth, many become enslaved by it, losing precious time and mental clarity in the process.

This spiritual degradation extends beyond the individual, affecting families and society at large. Our children—innocent and impressionable—who are particularly vulnerable are constantly exposed to a deluge of this spiritual pollution and have their *fitrah* (fih-trah), or natural disposition, distorted by the immoral content surrounding them. In a world where truth and virtue are portrayed as outdated, and vice is celebrated as freedom, we are called to engage in a jihad (spiritual struggle) against these forces. This is a battle for the soul, which requires mindfulness and a great deal of perspicacity and conscious action to realign with divine principles to protect our hearts and minds from being corrupted.

The modern world offers endless distractions and illusions, but truth remains unchanged. Those who consciously seek it, through divine guidance and inner discipline, will find clarity even in the midst of chaos. Islam and Taoism both teach that true fulfillment is not in grasping at the fleeting waves of the material world but in aligning oneself with the eternal flow of divine wisdom.

Halal consumption is used as a dietary guideline and as a form of worship and spiritual cleansing. Every morsel of halal food, the actions we take, and the environment to which we allow ourselves to be exposed become nourishment for the soul, raising us in spiritual awareness and bringing us closer to Allah. It is through such conscious living that we align with divine principles, fortifying ourselves against the moral decay that threatens our very essence. In the following passages, I would like to take you through the abhorrent conventional meat industry and some of its inhumane processes.

The Deep Cruelty of the Modern Meat Industry

What happens when we ignore divine and moral principles? The modern meat industry, driven by profit and greed, offers a chilling answer. Its cruelty knows no bounds, and its practices are a glaring violation of the sacredness of life. In this world of factory farming, the modern meat industry is nothing short of vile—a soulless machine prioritizing profit over the sanctity of life. It treats animals as mere commodities, stripping them of their dignity, while human workers become cogs in a machine that churns out suffering. This is not just an industry; it is a betrayal of our responsibility and sacred trust God has given us as stewards of life, dealing simultaneously with animal and human existence in ways that are both exploitative and inhumane. Animals are stripped of their dignity, reduced to mere products, and subjected to unimaginable suffering.

In the conventional meat industry, animals are raised in conditions that can only be described as abominable. Chickens, for example, are crammed into filthy sheds, with as many as 10,000 birds confined to less than two square feet each. The oppressive stench of ammonia fills the air, burning their lungs and eyes. These birds, swollen with hormones and antibiotics, struggle to support their own weight, their bodies buckling under unnatural growth. To prevent them from injuring one another in their misery, they are subjected to cruel mutilations—beak-trimming, de-spurring, dubbing, and sometimes de-toeing, all without anesthesia.

Cattle raised in the industrial meat and dairy industries endure severe physical and emotional suffering throughout their lives. From the start, they are subjected to painful mutilations without any anesthesia or pain relief. Branding with hot irons leaves second- and third-degree burns, causing pain that can last for months. Male calves are castrated and dehorned with no medical care, while dairy cows often undergo tail docking, impairing their ability to fend off flies and leaving them in chronic discomfort

In dairy operations, cows are kept in endless cycles of forced pregnancy and milk production. Calves are taken from their mothers within hours of birth, causing visible emotional distress as the mothers cry out and search for their offspring. Male calves are quickly slaughtered for veal, while female calves are destined to repeat the same grueling process. Over-milking leads to infections like mastitis, and some cows are injected with artificial hormones, such as rBST, which increases milk production but causes significant health problems.

Living conditions on factory farms are appalling. Cattle are confined to overcrowded feedlots, where they often stand in their own waste, breathing in ammonia-laden fumes that cause respiratory issues and skin diseases. Their diet, designed to fatten them quickly, consists mainly of corn and soy, which causes severe digestive problems, including fatal bloat and ulcers, as their bodies are not adapted to such feed.

The suffering continues during transport and slaughter. Cattle are crammed into trucks and driven for long distances without food, water, or rest, with many animals collapsing from heatstroke and exhaustion. In the slaughterhouses, despite regulations, ineffective stunning methods leave many animals conscious during the slaughter process. Cows, being social animals, recognize the death of their herd members. They experience intense fear and panic, often trying to escape as they watch others being killed in front of them. These animals are hung upside down, skinned, or dismembered alive while others watch, causing them extreme panic and distress.

Factory farming treats cattle as machines for profit rather than sentient beings capable of suffering. Their emotional well-being is ignored, even though cattle form strong bonds with their calves and herd mates. The relentless cycle of pain, confinement, and emotional trauma makes it clear that these animals endure immense cruelty at every stage of their lives. Awareness of these conditions is critical in promoting more humane practices and encouraging consumers to rethink their food choices.

Whether it is chickens, pigs, cattle, turkeys, ducks, fish, or lambs, the conditions in these industries mirror the same neglect, confinement, and cruelty seen with cattle and chickens. These creatures, meant to roam freely and live with dignity, are trapped in a nightmare from which there is no escape.

Here is a few examples of how slaughter is conventionally executed:

Stunning: A Façade of Humanity

Commercial slaughterhouses often employ stunning, a practice marketed as a humane way to kill. But this "humane" act is riddled with failure. Billions of animals are subjected to stunning each year—whether through blunt-force trauma, electrocution, or gassing. Yet too often, the process fails, leaving animals conscious and terrified as they are butchered alive.

Firearms and Captive Bolts: For cows, captive bolts are often used in place of bullets to render them unconscious. A thick piece of metal drives into the animal's brain, retracting back into the barrel. Yet, even this mechanical violence frequently fails. Up to 12.5% of cattle in the European Union remain conscious as they are hoisted upside down, their bodies trembling as their throats are slit. They meet their end not in peace but in terror, staring into the abyss of human cruelty. (The Human League, 2024)

Electrified Water Baths for Poultry: Birds fare no better. Chickens and turkeys, shackled upside down, are dragged through electrified water baths meant to stun them. Many survive the shock, fully aware of what comes next—the sharp blade that severs their throats. They feel everything: the burn of the water, the sting of the knife, and the weight of their helplessness.

Gas Chambers: The Silent Suffocation of Pigs

Pigs are known for their intelligence and emotional sensitivity. Studies have shown that pigs possess complex cognitive abilities, including long-term memory and an understanding of symbolic language. They are gassed with high concentrations of carbon dioxide. Trapped in metal cages and lowered into sealed chambers, they writhe in agony as the gas sears their lungs. Desperation consumes them as reports indicate that pigs gasp and thrash in panic as they slowly lose consciousness, they struggle for breath, thrashing violently against the cold metal bars. Some regain consciousness after the gas dissipates, only to be slaughtered fully awake, facing their end with wide, panicked eyes.

They can learn from observation and have shown empathy towards one another, demonstrating levels of intelligence comparable to that of a three-year-old human (Marino & Colvin, 2015). Despite these capacities, pigs on industrial farms are confined to cramped gestation crates, unable to turn around or express natural behaviors, leading to physical injuries and chronic pain due to prolonged time spent on hard floors (ASPCA, n.d.).

Don't worry, it gets worse. Once they have endured lifetimes of suffering, these animals begin their final, harrowing journey to the slaughterhouse. Herded onto crowded trucks or packed into cages, they are transported across vast distances. During the journey, many suffer from extreme weather—freezing cold or unbearable heat—while others succumb to exhaustion, hunger, or thirst. In the U.S. alone, 4 million chickens, 726,000 pigs, and 29,000 cattle die each year just in transit (The Human League 2024). Those who survive this torment arrive at the slaughterhouse, only to face their end in ways that defy any sense of compassion. The Prophet Muhammad (PBUH) reminded us, "Whoever is kind to the creatures of

God is kind to himself" (Bukhari). Yet this kindness is nowhere to be found in the industrial meat industry.

In Islamic teachings, the principle that animals should not witness the slaughter of other animals is rooted in the deep respect for all forms of life. This practice reflects not only compassion but also the understanding that animals, like humans, experience fear, stress, and emotional trauma. Recent studies on animal cognition have confirmed that animals can feel pain, fear, and anxiety, especially when exposed to the suffering of others in their vicinity. Witnessing the death of other animals can heighten their stress levels, causing them to release stress hormones, which accumulate in their tissues. This distress not only disrupts their well-being but also contradicts the values of mercy and dignity that Islam upholds in every aspect of life.

However, the rise of industrialized slaughterhouses has challenged this principle, as commercial meat production often involves mass processing where animals are killed in assembly-line conditions. Some Islamic scholars have issued rulings allowing mass commercial slaughter to accommodate the demand for halal meat in a globalized world. Yet, these rulings remain contentious, as they raise questions about whether such practices align with the deeper spirit of halal—a spirit rooted in compassion, respect, and mindfulness.

On a personal and spiritual level, I firmly believe that animals should never be subjected to the trauma of witnessing the slaughter of others. This principle is not merely about physical well-being but also addresses the energy and emotional states imprinted upon the animal at the time of death. In Islamic thought, there is an acknowledgment that what we consume affects us not just physically but spiritually. The flesh of an animal carries the energetic imprint of the life it lived. If an animal lived in constant states of anxiety, fear, and suffering, it is conceivable that these negative energies are absorbed into the bodies of those who consume its meat. According to Temple Grandin's article, "The Effect of Stress on Livestock and Meat Quality Prior to and During Slaughter," printed the *International Journal for the Study of Animal Problems* (1980), research supports the idea that the conditions under which animals are raised and slaughtered impact not only meat quality but also have potential implications for human well-being. Stress experienced by animals before and during slaughter has a significant effect on the biochemical composition of their meat.

When animals experience prolonged or acute stress—such as poor handling, extreme temperatures, or overcrowded transport—it alters their physiology, depleting muscle glycogen stores and causing abnormal pH levels in the meat. This results in tougher, less appetizing meat and compromises nutritional quality. Also, from a spiritual or energetic perspective, some traditions and holistic frameworks suggest that consuming meat from animals subjected to stress can transmit that "energy" to the consumer. While scientific research does not directly measure spiritual energy transfer, the stress hormones released by animals, such as cortisol, affect muscle tissue. When humans consume such meat, it's conceivable that residual stress hormones could impact bodily processes. Stress in animals correlates with reduced nutritional value and potential inflammatory effects in humans

This connection between the emotional state of animals and the energy we internalize through food invites a reflection on our collective well-being. Consider the possibility that the widespread consumption of meat from animals subjected to fear, pain, and trauma could contribute to the emotional imbalances increasingly prevalent in society. Could it be that the rising rates of anxiety, depression, and aggression among humans are not solely due to environmental or psychological factors but also a result of the energy we ingest from the food we consume?

In many ways, we are what we eat—not only in a physical sense but also in an emotional and spiritual sense. The Prophet Muhammad (PBUH) taught us to be mindful of our consumption, emphasizing that both the source and method of obtaining food have consequences on the soul. Eating animals that lived in suffering may influence our emotional state, amplifying negative emotions and distancing us from a state of inner peace and spiritual clarity. This understanding aligns with broader spiritual teachings found across various traditions, which emphasize the importance of purity in what we consume.

The halal requirements are not arbitrary rules—they are safeguards intended to preserve the well-being of both the consumer and the animal. Humane slaughter practices ensure that the animal experiences minimal suffering and that its death is meaningful and respectful. By adhering to these principles, we not only respect the animal but also protect ourselves from the potential harm of consuming suffering and negativity.

Consequently, the current practices in factory farming and slaughterhouses represent a grotesque disconnect from the sacred principles of halal. The assembly-line killing of animals treats them as commodities rather than living beings, robbing them of dignity and subjecting them to unbearable fear. This industrialized approach undermines the spiritual intent behind halal, reducing what should be a sacred act of consumption into a mechanical process driven by profit and efficiency. Research (Shultz, Hanover University, Germany) indicates the process of Halal slaughter involves very little pain (Schulze, 1978). Animals lose consciousness very quickly (typically within seconds), yet the heart pumps and helps to rid the body of blood. Professor Schultz and Dr. Hazim used an electrograph (EEG) and electrocardiogram (ECG) to prove the Islamic halal method is "the" humane way of slaughtering and captive bolt stunning practiced by the West causes severe pain to the animal.

Moving forward, it is essential to re-embrace the spirit of halal in its fullest sense—not only as a set of rules but as a way of living in harmony with all forms of life. By supporting ethical farming practices and mindful consumption, we can restore the balance between humanity and nature. Choosing to eat consciously—seeking out animals raised with care and slaughtered humanely—becomes not just an ethical decision but a spiritual act. It allows us to align our actions with divine guidance, creating peace within ourselves and acknowledging that every life, no matter how small, carries significance. By respecting this principle, we cultivate compassion and mindfulness, nurturing our souls while honoring the sacred trust given to us as stewards of the Earth.

The Environmental and Spiritual Catastrophe of Food Wastage

The horror doesn't end with the animals' deaths. The meat industry is not only cruel but deeply wasteful. A significant portion of this suffering is for nothing, as an alarming amount of food goes to waste. According to the USDA, globally, a staggering 1.3 billion tons of food—about one-third of all food produced—ends up wasted every year. In the U.S. alone, food waste accounts for 30-40% of the food supply, with over 119 billion pounds of perfectly edible food discarded annually (USDA 2023). This is more than just waste; it is an affront to the blessings we are given.

Each pound of wasted food represents the misuse of precious resources—water, energy, land—that were invested in producing that food. When food is wasted, so too is the labor of the farmers, the vitality of the soil, and the lives of the animals. The *Quran* reminds us of the gravity of wastefulness: "Indeed, the wasteful are brothers of the devils, and ever has Satan been to his Lord ungrateful" (Quran 17:27). Our culture of consumption without gratitude, of producing without purpose, has led us down a dangerous path.

Food wastage is also a major contributor to climate change. When food is discarded, it rots in landfills and emits methane, a potent greenhouse gas. According to the United Nations, food waste is responsible for 8-10% of global greenhouse gas emissions, driving the world ever closer to environmental catastrophe. The Prophet Muhammad (PBUH) warned us to "take from the earth only what is necessary," yet the modern world's addiction to overconsumption has led to mass destruction of the very planet that sustains us.

I would like you all to just think about it for a moment. I am sure that most of you have been witness to some amount of wastage, whether it be at your local grocery store or fast-food chain. I am sure that you have witnessed employees throwing away perfectly edible boxes of chicken, deli meats, or French fries.

One evening, my wife and I were at our local nationwide grocery store chain just as the deli was closing. Behind the counter, I noticed two large boxes stacked high with fried chicken—each box containing no less than 30 pieces. I pointed it out to my wife and said, "I bet all of that is going into the trash." She insisted I was wrong, unable to believe that so much perfectly good food would be wasted. To confirm, I asked the employee behind the counter what would happen to the chicken. She turned, gestured not only to the piles of chicken but to all the remaining food at the deli, and confirmed, "It all goes into the trash every night."

My wife was visibly shocked by this revelation. I could see the disbelief in her eyes, and to be honest, even though I knew it, hearing the confirmation still made my stomach turn. As I often do, I started quantifying the waste in real numbers.

To be optimistic, let's assume that only half of the 3,000 stores of this particular chain in the U.S. follow this practice—about 1,500 stores. If each store disposes of just one 30-piece box of chicken like the ones I saw (again, being conservative), that would mean 45,000 pieces of chicken were wasted per day.

Now, let's extend that number over the course of a year. If Walmart only wastes this much food half the days of the year (182 days), we would still be looking at over 8 million pieces of chicken discarded annually—from just one grocery chain. And this is just one type of food from one section of the store. Imagine expanding this estimate to all prepared food in all grocery stores across the country.

As I suspected, what we witnessed at Walmart wasn't an isolated incident. A 2018 report from the Natural Resources Defense Council (NRDC) found that supermarkets alone waste more than 43 billion pounds of food each year—a staggering amount, especially when you consider that millions of Americans face food insecurity.

Some businesses have implemented programs to donate unsold food, but many still discard vast amounts daily due to liability concerns, logistical issues, or simple policy failures. Programs like Feeding America and Food Rescue US work to redirect edible food to those in need, but the scale of waste remains overwhelming.

The sheer wastefulness of this system is hard to stomach. We could be redistributing excess food to shelters, food banks, and struggling families. We could be revising food safety policies to encourage donation instead of destruction. But instead, we bury edible food in landfills while hunger remains a daily reality for so many.

I want to believe my numbers are exaggerated—that I've miscalculated somewhere, and this crisis isn't as severe as it seems. But deep down, I know the reality is likely even worse when we account for all grocery stores, restaurants, and catering businesses across the country.

I hope that someday soon, we start treating food as the blessing it is—not as disposable waste. If we continue this trajectory, the environmental and spiritual consequences will be devastating. As ecosystems collapse, food prices rise, and hunger increases, we are reminded of the Prophet's words: "The earth is green and beautiful, and Allah has appointed you as His stewards over it" (Shaih Muslim). Yet we are failing in this duty, consuming the Earth's resources faster than it can replenish, all while throwing away the very sustenance that God has blessed us with.

Halal and Ethical Local Practices: A Call to Return to Balance

In the face of such destruction, the principles of halal offer a way out. By choosing halal and supporting ethical, local food production, we can begin to repair the damage we have caused. Halal is not just about the method of slaughter—it is about living with consciousness and care. When we embrace local food systems, we support farmers who prioritize animal welfare, environmental sustainability, and mindful consumption. The environmental benefits of these practices are significant. Choosing locally sourced food reduces the carbon footprint associated with long-distance transportation and overproduction, mitigating the strain on ecosystems. We break free from the industrial systems that treat life as disposable and instead cultivate a deep respect for the animals, land, and resources that sustain us.

Local and ethical farming practices embody the essence of *halal*—they prioritize the humane treatment of animals, ensure that food is produced sustainably, and reduce the wasteful practices that plague industrial farming. When animals are raised on small farms, they are allowed to graze, move freely, and live as nature intended. The contrast between this and the horrors of factory farming could not be more stark. When we consume locally, we are reminded of the direct relationship between the Earth's bounty and our own survival. Each meal becomes a moment of reflection, a chance to honor the cycle of life and death in a way that aligns with God's will.

The Prophet Muhammad (PBUH) taught us to "be mindful of your consumption, for every morsel of food is a blessing from Allah." By choosing ethical food sources, reducing waste, and supporting local production, we are living out this teaching in a way that benefits not only ourselves but the entire planet.

In a world dominated by waste, cruelty, and mindless consumption, the principles of *halal* serve as a beacon of hope, guiding us back to a life of balance, compassion, and gratitude. By embracing *halal* practices, we reject the cruelty of industrial farming, honor the sacredness of life, and commit to living in harmony with the Earth. The path of *halal* calls us to rise above the chaos of modern consumerism, to recognize that every choice we make—whether about food, behavior, or ethics—has spiritual consequences.

We must confront the realities of food wastage and industrial cruelty with a sense of urgency and moral responsibility. The choice is clear: continue the path of excess, destruction, and disregard, or return to the divinely ordained principles

Pork: The Unclean Truth

The prohibition of pork holds a unique place within the guidance offered by Islam, Judaism, and Christianity. Rooted in sacred teachings, it reflects a deeper concern for spiritual purity, physical health, and adherence to divine wisdom. In Islam, this prohibition is clear, "He has forbidden you blood and the flesh of swine, and that which has been dedicated to other than God." (Quran 2:173). Here, the swine's flesh is regarded as spiritually and physically impure, a substance unfit for consumption, as it represents a barrier between the body and spiritual well-being.

Similarly, in Judaism, dietary laws speak to the unclean nature of pork, as stated in Leviticus, "And the pig, because it parts the hoof and is cloven-footed but does not chew the cud, is unclean to you. You shall not eat any of their flesh, and you shall not touch their carcasses; they are unclean to you." (Leviticus 11:7–8). Such guidance emerges not merely from custom but from a sacred trust, a divine invitation to purity and health.

During Jesus' (PBUH) time, pork was strictly forbidden in accordance with Jewish dietary laws, as outlined in the Torah (Leviticus 11:7–8, Deuteronomy 14:8). Jesus himself adhered to these laws and never permitted pork consumption. It was later interpretations by his followers, particularly through Peter's vision (Acts 10:9–16) and Paul's teachings

(Romans 14:14), that led to the lifting of dietary restrictions for Gentile converts in the early Christian community.

By refraining from pork, followers of these paths seek to honor the Creator's intricate design of the human body and soul. In doing so, even their diet becomes a reflection of devotion, aligning one's actions with teachings that prioritize not just physical health but spiritual integrity. Increasingly, this wisdom is not limited to religious practice alone. A growing number of people—regardless of faith—are choosing to avoid pork purely for health and wellness reasons. Research has linked pork consumption to high levels of saturated fats and cholesterol, posing risks such as heart disease, obesity, and high blood pressure. Processed pork products like bacon and sausage have been classified as Group 1 carcinogens by the World Health Organization, placing them in the same category as tobacco for their link to colorectal cancer (WHO, 2015). Additionally, pigs are known carriers of parasites such as *Trichinella spiralis*, which can lead to trichinosis if the meat is undercooked or improperly handled. Many in the wellness and holistic communities also describe pork as a "low-vibrational" food—heavy on the body, clouding to the mind, and dulling to the spirit. These concerns, both scientific and energetic, serve as modern echoes of ancient wisdom, affirming that dietary choices are not merely matters of personal taste but consequences for body, mind, and soul. The Quran's guidance on this matter is not rooted in restriction but in preservation—a sacred alignment between what we consume and who we are becoming.

These teachings are more than dietary restrictions; they are calls to mindful living, honoring one's physical vessel as a trust from the divine. By choosing a diet that reflects this sanctity, individuals not only care for their health but also strengthen their spiritual alignment, recognizing the powerful connection between the material and the sacred. Through these practices, faith finds embodiment in action, guiding one toward a life of harmony, purity, and devotion.

"Do not think that I have come to abolish the Law or the Prophets; I have not come to abolish them but to fulfill them."
(Matthew 5:17)

Alcohol

In Islam, the prohibition of alcohol is not merely a restriction; it is a guiding principle toward a life of balance, awareness, and spiritual depth. Alcohol is recognized as a substance that can erode mental clarity, physical health, and spiritual growth. Islam places great emphasis on maintaining both physical and mental well-being, and alcohol, a depressant known to dull the senses, disrupts this harmony. The Quran warns of the consequences, acknowledging that while there may be some benefit in alcohol, its harm far outweighs it (Surah Al-Baqarah, Quran 2:219). Alcohol's potential to damage the body, impair judgment, and alter behavior makes it particularly detrimental to both individual and communal life.

Physiologically, alcohol impacts the central nervous system by slowing brain activity, earning its classification as a depressant—a categorization firmly grounded in pharmacology. It impairs cognitive functions, weakening decision-making abilities and leading individuals toward actions they may otherwise avoid. The World Health Organization (WHO) reports that alcohol contributes to nearly three million deaths globally each year, a staggering figure that accounts for about 5.3% of all fatalities worldwide. These tragic outcomes are linked not only to alcohol-related diseases, such as liver cirrhosis, cardiovascular issues, and various cancers, but also to accidents, injuries, and violence (World Health Organization, n.d.). The bodily toll is significant; alcohol places undue strain on vital organs, especially the liver and heart, which suffer greatly under its toxic effects.

The WHO's assertion that "there is no safe level of alcohol consumption" (World Health Organization, n.d.) echoes the Islamic teaching of complete abstention, highlighting that even moderate consumption introduces a degree of harm. Research from the US dietary guidelines reinforces this view, revealing that even within "safe" limits, alcohol increases risks for cancers and certain cardiovascular conditions (US Department of Health and Human Services, n.d.). Human biologist Gary Brecka states that alcohol metabolizes into acetaldehyde, a neurotoxin harmful to the body, illustrating how each drink subjects the body to toxic processes that hinder both physical health and mental clarity (Brecka, n.d.).

The growing trend in Western societies to reduce or eliminate alcohol consumption speaks to an emerging consciousness around wellness. Awareness campaigns, the popularity of non-alcoholic alternatives, and events centered on sober socializing reflect a collective shift toward moderation and health. Reports from the International Wines and Spirits Record (IWSR) and studies by organizations such as the National Institute on Alcohol Abuse and Alcoholism (NIAAA) illustrate the movement, with nearly 52% of adults in the US either reducing or attempting to reduce their intake (NIAAA, n.d.; IWSR, 2019). Many millennials, in particular, are embracing sobriety, redefining social norms with "dry bars" and alcohol-free gatherings that encourage connection without the risks associated with drinking (The Guardian, 2019; Forbes, 2019).

For Muslims, refraining from alcohol is a profound commitment to holistic health, self-discipline, and spiritual integrity. Abstinence preserves mental clarity, preserving the ability to make sound decisions and exercise restraint. Emotionally, it protects against impulsive behavior, aggression, and mood instability, creating a calm and balanced disposition conducive to self-reflection and personal growth. Alcohol, as a psychoactive substance, clouds judgment and can lead to actions that disrupt the harmony between body, mind, and spirit, moving individuals further from their divine purpose.

From a social perspective, the absence of alcohol promotes respectful and peaceful interactions, reducing conflicts, arguments, and misunderstandings. By choosing a path free from alcohol, Muslims aspire to create an environment of kindness, understanding, and mutual respect.

Spiritually, the decision to abstain from alcohol aligns with the higher pursuit of maintaining a clear channel to God. By avoiding substances that dull the senses and impair awareness, one remains fully attuned to the spiritual dimensions of life. Islam teaches that each choice—what we consume, how we act, and what we allow into our lives—impacts our journey toward closeness with the divine.

In Buddhist teaching, one of the five precepts warns against substances, like alcohol or drugs, that impair judgment and mindfulness (the other four focus on non-violence, honesty, sexual integrity, and avoiding theft). By refraining from intoxicants, Buddhists aim to maintain clarity, awareness, and self-control, reducing the likelihood of unskillful actions that could lead to harm. Both Judaism and Christianity both warn against the harms of excessive intoxication as well.

In Islam, living without alcohol is a conscious choice that cultivates a clear mind, a healthy body, emotional steadiness, and a grounded sense of purpose. It is a path that aligns with the divine call for balance and well-being, embracing life in its fullness without the distractions that lead to harm. Abstaining from alcohol is a reminder of the sacred responsibility Muslims carry to care for their bodies and souls, honoring the life they are given in a state of gratitude and awareness. In this pursuit of purity and purpose, one can achieve a fulfilling and purposeful existence anchored in clarity, compassion, and a deep spiritual connection with God.

The teachings of Islam, Taoism, and many other traditions emphasize that food should be a source of healing, balance, and spiritual elevation. Whether through avoiding impure substances like pork and alcohol, practicing moderation, or embracing mindful eating, conscious consumption deepens our connection with the divine and aligns us with our highest selves.

In a world of overindulgence, where food is often consumed mindlessly, returning to the sacred practice of eating with awareness and gratitude can transform not just our health but our entire spiritual experience.

By honoring what we consume, we honor ourselves, our Creator, and the natural flow of life—ensuring that our food nourishes not just our bodies but our souls.

JIHAD: A PATH OF INNER AND OUTER STRUGGLE

"God, grant me the serenity to accept the things I cannot change, courage to change the things I can, and the wisdom to know the difference."
–The Serenity Prayer

In the Western world, the term "jihad" is often portrayed by mainstream media in a distorted light, commonly depicting individuals calling for a "holy war" and inciting fear. However, this portrayal is a simplification that overlooks the depth and true meaning of jihad in Islam. The Arabic word "jihad" translates to "struggle" or "striving," derived from the root word "jahada," which means to exert effort. Within Islamic teachings, jihad encompasses a spectrum of meanings and contexts, foremost of which are the inner struggle to grow spiritually, self-mastery, resist temptation, and remain steadfast in faith.

In Taoism, the true battle is not against external enemies but against the chaos within. The path to self-mastery involves aligning oneself with the Tao (The Way), mastering inner energy (Qi), and dissolving the illusions of the ego.

At its core, jihad is the journey of refining the self. It is the everyday effort to live according to the principles of Islam, resisting one's own sinful desires and constantly working to purify one's heart and intentions. This personal struggle is known as the *greater jihad,* a lifelong commitment that calls believers to strive for inner peace, moral integrity, and a life of virtue. It includes a wide array of daily practices, such as prayer, patience, charity, and self-discipline, each seen as a building block in the pursuit of spiritual refinement and closeness to God.

The concept of jihad can also extend to the *outer struggle* for justice and defense. In specific and regulated circumstances, jihad may include the defense of one's community or homeland. However, even within this context, Islamic teachings emphasize clear restrictions, ethical conduct, and a deep aversion to harm or aggression toward innocents. The principles surrounding such situations aim to uphold justice, safeguard peace, and defend against oppression without violating the sanctity of life—a key value in Islam.

Interestingly, there is a profound correlation between the concept of jihad in Islam and the Christian notion of "bearing your cross." In Christianity, bearing one's cross symbolizes embracing life's difficulties, accepting burdens, and confronting adversity as part of a larger spiritual journey. It is about carrying life's responsibilities with grace and striving to overcome hardships with faith and endurance. Both concepts—jihad and bearing one's cross—call upon individuals to cultivate inner strength, patience, and resilience in the face of challenges. Similarly, Judaism's concepts of kiddush ha-Shem, yisurim, yetzer hara/yetzer hatov, tikkun olam, and enduring galut each echo themes of inner and outer struggle, sacrifice, and commitment to faith. While they may not have direct equivalents to jihad or bearing one's cross, these principles reflect similar values of endurance, moral struggle, and dedication to God's will.

By understanding these similarities, we see that jihad, Jewish concepts, and bearing one's cross encourage us to view hardships as opportunities for growth and spiritual fulfillment. Each concept acknowledges that personal struggles are integral to developing virtues like compassion, humility, and courage. Whether one approaches life's struggles as jihad or bearing their cross, these paths remind us that the journey toward righteousness, peace, and spiritual contentment demands resilience, sacrifice, and a steadfast commitment to truth and compassion.

Jihad and Taoist self-cultivation share common elements that transcend religious boundaries:

Overcoming the Ego: Islam's fight against the nafs aligns with Taoism's practice of dissolving attachment to self-importance.

Mastering the Mind: Both traditions emphasize mindfulness, meditation, and prayer as tools to refine thought and action.

Living with Purpose: The struggle of jihad and the Taoist path both advocate for living in harmony with divine purpose and natural law.

Serving Others: True mastery is not about personal gain but becoming a vessel of wisdom, compassion, and service.

By reframing jihad in its proper light, we reclaim its profound message of self-improvement, balance, and inner strength. Through internal struggle and spiritual refinement, one does not merely exist—one becomes.

True mastery begins with discipline—the ability to govern one's desires, refine one's actions, and align oneself with a higher order. The guidance in Islam regarding halal and haram, the discipline of jihad, and the abstention from intoxicants is not about restriction for the sake of hardship but about creating inner clarity, balance, and harmony. Similarly, Taoism teaches that alignment with the Tao (The Way) requires purification, moderation, and self-awareness, ensuring that one's energy flows unimpeded by excess or impurity.

The wisdom behind these principles lies in their ability to elevate the human being beyond mere indulgence and impulse. To refrain from harmful substances like alcohol and pork is not simply an external practice but a spiritual discipline that ensures one remains pure in body, mind, and soul. In Taoist thought, stagnation leads to decay, and just as a river must flow to remain pure, so must our habits and actions remain free from corruption. Jihad, in its truest sense, is this struggle—the continuous refinement of the self, the effort to overcome the lower tendencies that hinder spiritual growth. This mirrors the Taoist principle of *neidan* (internal alchemy), where one transforms the base elements of nature into something more refined, more harmonious, and more enlightened.

The battle against excess, indulgence, and heedlessness is not fought in a single moment but in every decision we make. The foods we consume, the struggles we engage in, and the disciplines we uphold are all part of a greater movement toward self-mastery and divine connection. To live by these principles is not simply to follow the rules but to embody a way of life that brings about clarity, balance, and alignment with the natural and spiritual order.

Islam and Taoism both remind us that life is a flowing current, and those who align themselves with its natural order will find peace and strength. By consuming mindfully, struggling consciously, and refining our intentions, we do not simply live—we thrive, evolve, and draw nearer to the divine. The path is before us, clear and unwavering. The choice is ours—to remain stagnant or to walk the journey of transformation, embracing the wisdom of discipline, self-purification, and balance.

"On your journey, flow like the water which takes all forms: rivers into lakes, lakes into oceans, oceans into raindrops. Still, never relinquish your quintessential truth, core, and essence, for when you arrive at source it will show that you were always on course." –Ah Lee

WOMEN OF ISLAM

"The world and all things in it are precious, but the most precious thing in the world is a righteous woman."
(Sunan Ibn Majah 1855, Sahih Muslim 1467)

Women in Islam are deeply significant in the faith's spiritual and social fabric. However, their positions are often obscured by misconceptions, leading many to mistakenly believe that Islam itself condones the mistreatment or oppression of women. In reality, Islam advocates for kindness, respect, and compassion toward women, affirming their dignity and fundamental equality. Islam declares that all human beings, regardless of gender, possess an intrinsic worth. Both men and women are considered equally accountable before Allah, with shared rights and responsibilities that arise from their shared humanity. This focus on equality is rooted in Islam's foundational texts, the Quran and Hadith, which laid out protections and rights for women that were groundbreaking in the 7th century, especially compared to the norms in Jewish and Christian societies of the time.

Another common reason some perceive Islam as oppressive to women lies in the cultural practices of Eastern countries, which often differ significantly from those of the West. In many Eastern societies, family-centered living is highly valued, and women, particularly mothers, often take on the primary responsibility for household duties such as nurturing children, managing the home, cooking, and providing a stable environment. Meanwhile, men traditionally focus on earning an income to support the household.

While the mistreatment of women does occur in some Muslim-majority societies, it's crucial to understand that these instances stem from cultural practices rather than the core teachings of Islam. Islam, like any major religion, has historically been interwoven with a variety of cultural interpretations and local customs, which at times distort or even contradict its fundamental values. But to attribute such injustices to the religion itself is to overlook the essence of Islamic guidance, which strongly emphasizes equality and human dignity. Islam's core values seek to honor, uplift, and protect women in family and society. By clearly distinguishing these religious teachings from cultural practices that may vary across societies, we can appreciate Islam's revolutionary approach in establishing women's rights well before many other traditions.

The Quran itself underscores the importance of women's rights and recognizes their indispensable role in family, community, and faith. It encourages the active participation of women in all aspects of life, affirming that their spiritual, intellectual, and social contributions are as valuable as those of men. Any notion that Islam limits or oppresses women is fundamentally at odds with the message of the Quran, which calls for a respectful and equitable treatment of all.

In 7th-century Arabia, Islamic law introduced progressive rights for women in areas such as inheritance, property ownership, marital consent, divorce, education, and financial independence. Islam was one of the earliest systems to codify and introduce reforms to rights, often exceeding those available to women in Jewish and Christian societies at the time. Islam's emphasis on justice, protection, and dignity for women established a revolutionary legal foundation, recognizing women as independent individuals with distinct rights and contributions to society.

To be clear, the unjust treatment of women in some societies is not an Islamic teaching but a deviation shaped by cultural practices. Islam, at its core, upholds the principles of justice, equality, and respect for every individual. This understanding is paramount in separating cultural influences from actual religious teachings. In Islam, a woman's value is not diminished; rather, it is honored, her role is cherished, and her rights are protected. By distinguishing between these cultural norms and authentic Islamic values, we can see that Islam's true essence is one that uplifts, supports, and empowers women.

This legal protection was progressive for 7th-century Arabia, where women often had no inheritance rights. While Jewish and Christian traditions had some inheritance laws, in pre-Islamic Arabia, local tribal customs often overruled these laws, leaving many women without a rightful share. The Quranic reforms set a new legal precedent that significantly improved women's financial security in the region. By affirming their right to financial security, Islam promoted women's autonomy and independence in ways that influenced legal systems beyond Islamic societies. Islam's inheritance laws marked a shift toward inclusivity and gender justice. Other societies granted women inheritance rights only much later, underscoring Islam's pioneering stance on economic rights for women.

Here are some more key aspects highlighting the importance and reverence given to women in Islam.

Right to Own Property and Wealth

Islam granted women the right to own, inherit, and manage property independently, allowing them to engage in business, own land, and retain full control over their wealth before and after marriage. Khadijah, the first wife of the Prophet Muhammad (PBUH), exemplified this independence as a wealthy and successful businesswoman who retained full control over her wealth.

Right to Dowry (Mahr)

Islam established the concept of mahr, a mandatory gift from the husband to the wife at the time of marriage. This dowry becomes the wife's personal property, serving as financial security for her. The Quran reinforces this, stating, "And give the women (upon marriage) their [bridal] gifts graciously..."(Quran 4:4)

Right to Consent in Marriage

Islam emphasizes the right of women to accept or reject marriage proposals, making their consent a necessary condition for a valid marriage. Forced marriages are considered invalid under Islamic law. A hadith narrates that a woman approached the Prophet Muhammad to annul a marriage arranged without her consent, and he upheld her right to choose.

Right to Divorce

In Islam, women have the right to seek divorce (khula) through a legal process. Additionally, women retain specific financial rights after divorce, such as a waiting period (iddah) during which their ex-husband must support them. (Quran 2:229) outlines these provisions, granting women autonomy in marital separation.

Right to Education

Islam strongly encourages both men and women to seek knowledge. The Prophet Muhammad declared, "Seeking knowledge is an obligation upon every Muslim" (Sunan Ibn Majah). This emphasis on education is further exemplified by prominent women in Islamic history, such as Aisha bint Abu Bakr, a renowned scholar who transmitted thousands of hadiths, and Fatima al-Fihri, the founder of the world's first university.

Right to Work and Earn Income

Islam permits women to work and earn an income, emphasizing that their earnings belong solely to them. Financial support for the household is the husband's responsibility, leaving women free to manage their finances independently.

Right to Personal Dignity and Protection Against Harm

Islam established principles to protect women from harm, oppression, and exploitation. Men are instructed to treat women with kindness, and husbands are expected to care for and provide for their wives. emphasizes, "… live with them in kindness." (Quran 4:19)

I am only pointing out that Islam, the religion itself, does not endorse or condone subjugation towards women; rather, it places high regard and emphasizes respect, love, and care towards women. There are even several hadiths that specify that women have sexual rights over their husbands, and they are entitled to be sexually satisfied by their husbands and must not be neglected.

The dynamic, collaborative partnership, where the husband's financial contributions complement the wife's management and nurturing of the family, is a sound foundation for providing a favorable environment for raising a family. In this structure, the man often assumes the role of guiding and directing the family while his wife consults, advises, and supports his leadership—a balance that fosters unity and strength within the family unit.

To me, this model represents a beautiful synergy. It allows both partners to contribute their unique strengths to the family's success and well-being. However, in many Western societies, the emphasis is on shared responsibilities both in the workplace and at home. Women are encouraged—often out of necessity—to join the workforce and divide household duties equally with their spouses. While this approach aligns with cultural values of equality, it sometimes places undue pressure on women to excel in multiple roles simultaneously, creating challenges in maintaining balance.

It is my personal belief that men and women, while equal in their value and rights, are not identical in their capacities. Beyond the obvious anatomical differences, men and women often exhibit distinct emotional tendencies, stress responses, spatial abilities, and behavioral patterns. These differences are complementary, not hierarchical. By acknowledging them, societies can create structures that play to the strengths of both genders.

Several contemporary studies and organizations indicate that a significant number of women prefer to stay home and raise their families rather than engage in full-time employment. This preference is influenced by various factors, including personal fulfillment, family well-being, and societal expectations.

- Gallup Poll (2015): A Gallup poll revealed that 56% of American mothers with children under 18 would prefer to stay home over working outside the home.
- Pew Research Center (2014): The Pew Research Center reported an increase in stay-at-home mothers, noting that more than one in four mothers in the U.S. were stay-at-home moms as of 2014.
- Institute for Family Studies (2020): Research from the Institute for Family Studies found that stay-at-home mothers often experience high levels of satisfaction in their role, valuing the opportunity to focus on family care.
- Mother Untitled: Founded by Neha Ruch, Mother Untitled is a community that supports women choosing to pause or adjust their careers to focus on family. The platform provides resources and narratives to empower women in their decision to prioritize child-rearing during certain phases of life.

Furthermore, I hold that no role is more vital or elevated than that of a mother or homemaker. A mother's contributions go beyond the tangible; she is often the foundation of a family's sanctuary, crafting a space of peace, stability, and love. This sanctuary allows family members to recharge from the stresses and demands of life—a respite from the often-daunting tasks of work, school, and external obligations. In a world full of demands, disappointments, and challenges, the home, lovingly cultivated by a mother or homemaker, becomes a haven of solace and restoration. It is this role, full of dignity and purpose, that should be celebrated and honored as indispensable to the health and harmony of both the family and society at large. Prophet Muhammad's last sermon included the treatment of women, "O People, it is true that you have certain rights over your women, but they also have rights over you. Treat your women well and be kind to them, for they are your partners and committed helpers."

Sanctuary of Mother

In the quiet morning light, she wakes,
As dawn gently whispers, nature stirs and shakes.
With tender hands, she tends to blooming flowers,
Crafting a sanctuary with her loving powers.

Her heart, a garden where wildflowers grow,
Each petal caressed by morning's golden glow.
She sows seeds of peace in every room,
Transforming a house into a fragrant bloom.

The birds' songs echo her gentle voice,
In her presence, the children rejoice.
A mother's touch, like soft spring rain,
Nourishing souls, easing every pain.

She weaves the sunlight through the trees,
Breathing life into the gentle breeze.
Her prayers, like a river's song,
Guiding her family, keeping them safe and strong.

In her embrace, a forest deep,
Where her families' dreams are in safety's keep.
Her love, like roots of ancient oak,
Steady and strong, in an enamored cloak.

She crafts a home with tender care,
A sanctuary, serene and rare.
Where husbands find his burdens light,
In her warmth, the darkest night.

She orchestrates a meal with love's pure grace,
A nurturing haven, a welcoming place.
Her husband, tired from the day's long quest,
Finds peace and comfort, a place to rest.

She listens to his worries, his silent pleas,
With wisdom born of ancient trees.
Together they build a sacred space,
A home filled with love, a divine embrace.

Her role, a symphony of nature's grace,
Creating a haven, a sacred space.
With every breath, with every prayer,
She builds a world of love and care.

Oh mothers, keepers of life's flame,
Unsung heroes, by any name.
In the garden of our lives, they stand,
A testament to love, which no evil can withstand.

Their presence, a gentle summer's breeze,
A balm to hearts, a soul's sweet ease.
In their hands, the world feels right,
A sanctuary of love, in the soft twilight.
—Ah Lee

Here is a list of Muslim women who have served in notable government positions in their respective countries:

- Benazir Bhutto: Prime Minister of Pakistan (1988–1990 and 1993–1996)
- Khaleda Zia: Prime Minister of Bangladesh (1991–1996 and 2001–2006)
- Tansu Çiller: Prime Minister of Turkey (1993–1996)
- Sheikh Hasina: Prime Minister of Bangladesh (1996–2001 and 2009–present)
- Mame Madior Boye: Prime Minister of Senegal (2001–2002)
- Megawati Sukarnoputri: President of Indonesia (2001–2004)
- Roza Otunbayeva: President of Kyrgyzstan (2010–2011)
- Atifete Jahjaga: President of Kosovo (2011–2016)
- Cissé Mariam Kaïdama Sidibé: Prime Minister of Mali (2011–2012)
- Sibel Siber: Prime Minister of Northern Cyprus (2013)
- Aminata Touré: Prime Minister of Senegal (2013–2014)
- Ameenah Gurib-Fakim: President of Mauritius (2015–2018)
- Halimah Yacob: President of Singapore (elected in 2017)
- Samia Suluhu Hassan: President of Tanzania since 2021, notable as the country's first female head of state
- Fatima al-Fihri: Founded the University of al-Qarawiyyin in the 9th century, recognized as one of the world's oldest universities.
- Aisha bint Abu Bakr(PBUH): Early Islamic scholar and authority in Islamic jurisprudence, contributing significantly to religious teachings.

THE QURAN: A LIGHT FOR THE PATH

"Blessed are the peacemakers, for they shall be called
the children of God. (Matthew 5:9)

The Quran is not simply the holy book of Islam—it is the very soul of the religion. It is the unaltered, unfiltered word of Allah, sent down to humanity through the heart of the Prophet Muhammad (PBUH), a man chosen not for wealth, power, or prestige, but for purity of character and depth of trust. Over twenty-three years, in moments of silence and battle, in nights of prayer and the heat of social resistance, the Quran descended—verse by verse, chapter by chapter—into the human world. It is divine revelation—not authored, not assembled, but revealed.

For Muslims, the Quran is more than a book—it is a lifelong companion. It holds the answers not only to theological questions but to the questions every soul asks when alone, in crisis, or in search of purpose. It teaches about prayer, how to forgive, how to fight with justice, how to surrender with grace. Its verses do not age. They remain eternally relevant because they speak to the deepest realities of the human condition: the search for meaning, the battle with ego, the longing for peace, and the pull toward God.

In Islam, guidance is not limited to moral suggestions. It is a divine right granted to every human being—the chance to know their Lord and walk the path of truth. The Quran is that path. It doesn't only direct from a distance; it walks beside you. In times of joy, it reminds you of gratitude. In hardship, it reminds you of patience. In loss, it calls you back to tawakkul—complete trust in God. It builds a worldview that is not swayed by trends, nor broken by trials. It teaches balance: between body and soul, dunya and akhirah, strength and humility.

Every verse of the Quran is layered. There is the surface meaning accessible to all. Then there is the inward meaning, which opens with reflection, sincerity, and prayer. It was designed this way—revealed gradually, with deliberate rhythm and context—because the human heart doesn't transform overnight. It needs time, repetition, softness, and struggle. And the Quran meets the believer where they are. A child may find comfort in it. A scholar may spend a lifetime on a single chapter. A sinner may find the first verse they read opens the door to their return.

It is recited in prayer not simply as tradition, but because its sound itself is healing, (*Faris & Tahir, 2022, Frontiers in Psychiatry*). Its Arabic flows not just through the tongue but through the cells. It calms the nervous system, realigns intention, and brings awareness back to the divine. Even those who do not understand its words can feel its weight when recited. The Quran is a vibration. A frequency that carries remembrance into the world. And wherever it is sincerely read, the atmosphere shifts.

But the Quran is not passive. It challenges. It demands introspection, accountability, and submission—not to fear, but to the Creator who shaped the soul and set it free. It speaks against injustice, arrogance, and heedlessness. It stands for the oppressed. It warns those who manipulate truth. It speaks not only of heaven and hell, but of the daily battle between light and darkness inside the self.

To be a Muslim is to live in dynamic relationship with the Quran. It is to visit it daily—not always with understanding, but always with reverence. It is to allow it to mold your ethics, soften your character, and sharpen your perception. It is to trust that even in the hardest verses, there is wisdom. Even in the simplest phrases, there is eternity.

In a world of shifting values and temporary truths, the Qur'an remains unmoved. It is not a document of the past. It is the living Word of the Eternal, guiding the heart that is ready to listen. For those who truly seek, it becomes everything: mirror, map, anchor, and key. The light upon light. The rope that never frays. The voice that never fades.

Let the Quran not simply be read. Let it be absorbed. Let it be lived. Let it be the sound that follows you in silence, the compass when you lose direction, the medicine when the world feels too loud. For those who walk with it, the path does not disappear. The One who revealed it never leaves.

CLOSING

"A person is either your brother in faith or your equal in humanity."
–Imam Ali

Too often, religion is reduced to an identity—something one inherits rather than embodies. But Islam was never meant to be a mere label. It is a path, a journey, a state of being that calls for continuous growth, refinement, and surrender to the divine. To be Muslim is not just to profess belief but to walk in harmony with divine will and to cultivate righteousness in every thought, action, and breath. In this way, Islam is not a stagnant title; it is a living, breathing practice—a road that is walked, not just a name that is claimed.

This mirrors the essence of Taoism, where the Tao (The Way) is not something one simply believes in, but something one lives through. Just as the Tao cannot be truly defined—only experienced—Islam, too, is realized through devotion, action, and sincerity. Both traditions teach that true understanding comes not from labels or rigid adherence to form but through alignment with divine order and conscious embodiment of truth.

In Islam, the Sirat al-Mustaqim (the Straight Path) is the road to divine guidance and ultimate fulfillment. It is not merely a destination but an ongoing discipline—a commitment to justice, truth, and balance in all aspects of life. Every prayer, every decision, every struggle is a step forward on this path, requiring both faith and effort.

In Taoism, the Tao (The Way) is the underlying order of the universe, the natural flow that one must attune to in order to find peace and wisdom. To fight against the Tao is to live in resistance, but to flow with it is to exist in harmony. The same truth applies to Islam's Sirat al-Mustaqim—it is not merely about external observance but about spiritual alignment, humility, and trust in divine wisdom.

Both concepts share an essential truth: the path is not rigid but dynamic. It requires surrender, adaptability, and the willingness to walk it anew each day. The straight path does not mean a life without struggle, just as flowing with the Tao does not mean passivity—it means navigating life with wisdom, balance, and a heart attuned to the divine. Islam is like a river with strong banks—it has clear boundaries, but within those banks, the water flows, moves, adapts, and carves its own path.

Both traditions, Islam and Tao, emphasize that the true path is not something external to be memorized but something internal to be lived. It is a way of moving, seeing, and being—one that requires discipline, reflection, and trust in the unseen.

It is my hope that this work has illuminated a new perspective on the essence of Islam—or the *Tao of Islam*—and that it has nurtured a deeper connection to your own spiritual beliefs. To my Hindu, Buddhist, Jewish, Christian, non-denominational, and Muslim brothers and sisters—and to the agnostic and atheist souls still searching in the dark or standing firm in doubt—I offer this: May we lean into the light that binds us, not the shadows that divide us. As diverse as the colors of a rose garden, we are all bound by our shared humanity and devotion to a singular Creator who watches over us with infinite love.

Islam teaches us that diversity in faith, culture, and practice is not a barrier to unity but an invitation to compassion and understanding. The Quran beautifully captures this in its verses:

"To every person We have appointed rites and ceremonies which they must follow; let them not dispute with you on the matter, but do invite them to your Lord, for you are assuredly on the right way. If they do wrangle with you, say: 'God knows best what it is you are doing'" (Quran 76:69).

"For you is your religion, and for me is my religion" (Quran 109:6).

"We have appointed a law and a practice for every one of you—had God willed, He would have made you a single community, but He wanted to test you regarding what has come to you. So compete with each other in doing good. Every one of you will return to God, and He will inform you regarding the things about which you differ" (Quran 48).

These verses remind us that while we may walk different paths, our ultimate goal is the same: to strive for goodness and return to the Creator, who knows our hearts.

It is not my intention to impose my beliefs or claim superiority of one faith over another. Rather, it is my heartfelt desire to share the sublime beauty of Islam as I understand it and to bridge the commonalities among humanity's diverse spiritual traditions. We are one family, united by the belief in a Creator who cherishes us all. Just as the sun shines equally on all living things, so does God's mercy extend to each of us, regardless of our creed.

I humbly acknowledge that my understanding of the Quran comes through translation and personal interpretation, and I approach it with a heart open to its wisdom. Despite any controversial verses or differing interpretations, I am deeply inspired by the discipline and spiritual framework that Islam provides. The Five Pillars of Islam resonate as profound acts of devotion, self-improvement, and service.

The act of praying five times daily (salat) instills gratitude and mindfulness, anchoring the believer in the remembrance of God throughout the day. Fasting (sawm) during Ramadan is not just a physical discipline but a powerful spiritual exercise that teaches self-control and compassion for those less fortunate. Giving in charity (zakat) imprints a sense of interconnectedness and responsibility, ensuring that wealth circulates to uplift the community. The pilgrimage (hajj) to Mecca is a transformative journey of self-discovery and unity, reminding us of our shared origin and destiny. Declaring faith (shahada) in the Creator and submitting to the will of God provides a sense of purpose and accountability, inviting us to live in alignment with a higher truth.

Contrary to misconceptions that Islam is a rigid or unforgiving faith, its essence is steeped in mercy and compassion. Every chapter of the Quran begins with the words "Bismillahir Rahmanir Rahim," which means "In the name of God, the Most Compassionate, the Most Merciful." This constant invocation of God's mercy reminds us that His forgiveness is vast, His love unbounded, and His compassion ever-present.

To my Muslim brothers and sisters and to all who feel distant from the divine, I urge you not to shy away from God. If your heart is heavy with guilt or regret, if you feel unworthy of grace, know that God's mercy is greater than your despair. Turn to Him, seek refuge in His compassion, and unburden your soul. There is no sin too great, no mistake too deep, that cannot be absolved by the One whose mercy encompasses all things. As the great Denzel Washington so eloquently put it: "I've been protected, I've been directed, I've been corrected. I've kept God in my life, and it's kept me humble. I didn't always stick with him, but he always stuck with me."

Think about it—five times a day, you're invited into a ritual that aligns you with the universe. An obligation, but not for anyone else's benefit but yours. Five times a day, you cleanse your body and energy. You step into meditation, reset your mind, ground yourself in gratitude, and move through a flow that subtly strengthens you—a built-in wellness system centuries ahead of its time.

Once a year, you embark on a full-body reset—fasting, detoxing, and recalibrating your rhythms with nature's pulse. You detach from excess, silence distractions, and reawaken your instincts.

You're obligated to give, not as charity but as a spiritual practice—zakat isn't about a transaction; it's about transformation. It keeps your heart light, your ego in check, and your connection to humanity intact.

And if you're able, at least once in your life, you take a pilgrimage—not a vacation, not a retreat, but a journey into the deepest currents of ancient wisdom, where you walk the same sacred paths as millions before you, absorbing a tradition so vast it defies time itself.

Islam isn't just a religion—it's a highly evolved spiritual technology, a system designed for peak existence. It's like Taoism but with blueprints, structure, and a built-in rhythm that keeps you in sync with yourself and the cosmos.

Think about it—this isn't just faith, it's flow.

Islam teaches us that God is not a distant figure to be feared but a loving Creator who welcomes those who seek Him. As the Quran states:

"Say, O My servants who have transgressed against themselves [by sinning], do not despair of the mercy of Allah. Indeed, Allah forgives all sins. Indeed, it is He who is the Forgiving, the Merciful" (Quran 39:53).

The beauty of Islam lies in its ability to transform lives through devotion, discipline, and compassion. It invites believers to walk a path of service, to uplift others, and to strive for personal growth. Go through the motions of prayer, and your heart will find solace. Fast with intention, and your spirit will be strengthened. Give in charity, and you will feel the ripple of goodness in your soul and community. Embark on a pilgrimage, and you will discover the depths of your being and your connection to the divine.

I firmly believe that the Creator, in His infinite wisdom and compassion, values the sincerity of our actions over the labels we assign ourselves. If you live a life of kindness, service, and gratitude, how could the divine ever deny you the rewards of a life well-lived? The law of the universe seems to echo this truth: goodness begets goodness, and those who strive for harmony will find peace.

I urge us, regardless of faith or background—to embrace our shared humanity and to live lives that reflect the values of compassion, justice, and unity. Let us strive to do good for one another, for in serving others, we serve the Creator. And let us always remember that the light of God shines within each of us, waiting to be kindled into a flame that can illuminate the world.

As we reach the conclusion of this journey, it is essential to recognize that the pursuit of truth does not end here. Spiritual awakening is not a singular moment but a continuous unfolding, a lifelong alignment with the divine reality. Islam and Taoism, though distinct in form, both guide the seeker toward the same ultimate truth—a return to the One.

To live in harmony with this deeper understanding, one must integrate spiritual wisdom into daily existence. This means embracing mindful presence, surrendering to the divine flow, and embodying compassion and service. True faith is not found in mere rituals alone but in the transformation of the heart, in the way one interacts with the world and with others.

Every moment, every action, and every breath can become an act of devotion when carried out with divine consciousness. Just as the Taoist master aligns with the natural order, the sincere believer aligns with the will of Allah, finding peace not in control but in submission to the higher wisdom.

The end of a book is not the end of the journey—it is only a transition to the next stage. The knowledge shared here is not meant to be passively absorbed but actively engaged with, questioned, and applied. The true seeker never ceases to seek; they walk the path with humility, curiosity, and an open heart.

No spiritual system can be reduced to mere words on a page, for truth is a living reality—one that must be experienced, tested, and internalized. Whether through prayer, contemplation, service, or study, each individual must find their own way to deepen their connection to the divine.

Let this be a reminder that spirituality is not confined to books, places of worship, or rigid doctrines—it is the undercurrent of existence itself, flowing through all things. It is in every sunrise, every breath, and every act of kindness. It is in the stillness of the heart when it truly remembers its origin.

And so, the journey does not end—it continues with each step you take toward truth, wisdom, and the eternal light of the divine.

May you walk this path with sincerity, strength, and an unwavering heart.

The path remains open. The call to return is eternal. The choice to walk it is yours.

"There are no rules for worship.
He will hear the voice of every heart that is sincere." –Rumi

APPRECIATION AND
ACKNOWLEDGMENTS

"Learn lessons from fools and sages alike, for there is always wisdom to discern." –Ah Lee

Thank you to the voices I never met—the authors, fighters, philosophers, truth-speakers, and troublemakers. You cracked open doors I didn't know I was allowed to walk through. In your courage, I found language. In your defiance, I found backbone. You were the mentors I didn't have in the room, the fire I needed when everything around me felt cold.

But I also want to thank the real ones—the people in my life who, whether by intention or accident, helped shape me. The ones who didn't always have the right word, but gave me something solid to hold onto. Whether you lifted me, challenged me, loved me, or even walked away—you helped me grow.

Growth doesn't always come from comfort. Sometimes, it comes from collision, silence, or distance. But to all of you—near or far, loud or quiet— thank you. Every voice, every lesson, every scar helped carve the person behind these pages.

This book is part testimony, part thank-you letter, part offering. And every line of it carries you in it.

I also want to acknowledge something that might be obvious to some— my list of appreciations includes individuals who are controversial, polarizing, and in some cases may not align with Islamic values or beliefs. I am fully aware that many of these figures hold views or have lived lives I do not fully endorse. But I choose to honor the parts of them that lit a path for me—the fragments of brilliance, courage, and insight that helped me grow. As I've shared throughout this book, I focus on what uplifts and strengthens my spirit, and I let the rest fall away.

There is wisdom to be gathered even from those we differ with. We do not need to agree on everything to respect what someone has offered. I have learned from both the devout and the doubtful, from the humble and the arrogant, from the healed and the hurting. And I believe we can hold space for complexity without collapsing into hatred. Spiritual growth demands discernment—but also compassion. I choose to focus on the parts that inspire, that elevate, that remind me of God's presence in even the most unlikely places. The rest, I leave.

Because we are not here to divide one another by labels, but to learn, reflect, and uplift. And sometimes, the most sacred guidance is found in the most unexpected vessels. Because wisdom doesn't always come dressed in perfection. And sometimes the most powerful lessons arrive from unexpected teachers.

- Muhammad Ali - Heavyweight Boxing Champion/ Philosopher - Thank you for being the best fighter that I have witnessed in my life and being a good force in the world and defiant in the face of wrongful persecution. RIP
- Mike Tyson - Heavyweight Boxing Champion - Thank you for being a ferocious motivator and philosopher.
- Bruce Lee - Martial artist/ Author/ Philosopher - Thank you for proving what dedication can evolve into. RIP
- Joe Rogan - Comedian/ Philanthropist/ Bad Ass - Thank you for adding eloquence into the art of combat and pushing the envelope for open dialog, for being part philosopher, part fighter, part force of nature, and for being a seeker not a preacher.
- Khabib Nurmagomedov - UFC Champion - Thank you for showing the world what it means to be a humble champion, embodying discipline, unbreakable faith, and advocating for Islam.

- Islam Makhachev – Thank you for carrying on a legacy of humility and brotherhood.
- Andrew Tate III – Thank you for bravery and stepping outside the matrix and reaching back pull others out, pushing resilience, discipline, and self-mastery.
- Tristian Tate – Thank you for being the brother every brother needs.
- James Allen – Thank you for distilling timeless truth into quiet wisdom.
- Lex Fridman – Thank you for your efforts build bridges and understanding.
- Candace Owens – Thank you for bravery and perusing truth, your righteousness, speaking fearlessly, challenging the narrative, and being a force for the Almighty.
- Eckhart Tolle – Thank you for reminding me that presence is power, and that silence often speaks louder than the ego ever could. Your words helped me unhook from the noise and return to the stillness where truth lives.
- Noam Chomsky – Thank you for your relentless pursuit of truth, your courage to speak it plainly, and your lifelong resistance to the machinery of manufactured consent. Your clarity has helped me see through illusion and question the narratives we're told to accept.
- George Orwell – Thank you for daring to write what others were too afraid to even think. Your vision cut through illusion and named the quiet tyrannies that still wear new faces. You reminded me that clarity is rebellion, and language is a battlefield.
- Tucker Carlson – Thank you for your patriotism and your passion for truth.
- Jeffery Sachs – Thank you for championing for peace.
- Roger Waters – Thank you for turning sound into resistance and grief into anthems. Your voice has always cut through the static, challenging the machinery, mourning the madness, and calling out

to whatever's left of our collective conscience. You reminded me that art isn't just for feeling - it's for remembering, resisting, and waking up.

- Mehdi Hasan – Thank you for wielding words like a surgeon, cutting through spin, evasion, and double-speak. Your clarity, conviction, and unwillingness to bow to power reminded me that truth, when spoken with courage, is a form of worship.
- Dr. Zakir Naik – Thank you for sharing your knowledge of Islam and the Quran.
- Malcom X – Thank you for your courage, wisdom, integrity, and revolutionary spirit.
- Dave Smith – Thank you for sharp wit, logic, patriotism, and unwavering principles.
- David Goggins – Thank you for proving that the mind is the ultimate battleground and limits are meant to be broken.
- Reza Arslan – Thank you for insightful storytelling and bridging history with faith.
- Karen Armstrong – Thank you for bridging faith and history.
- Hassan Minhaj - Thank you for turning laughter into insight, carving out space for your story, and making the personal profoundly political without losing your heart.
- Dan Bilzerian - Thank you for being a reflection of the untamed, and a reminder that even in a world of noise, there's discipline behind the scenes and intention beneath the image. For being a walking contradiction and somehow a mirror of the times. You made me question excess, masculinity, freedom, and illusion—all in the same scroll.
- Norman Finkelstein – Thank you for your fearless scholarship and unwavering commitment to justice and truth.
- Khalil Gibran – Thank you for poetic wisdom, timeless beauty in words, and spiritual depth that transcends generations. RIP

- Jalal Ad-Din Muhammad Rumi – Thank you for your divine poetry, endless wisdom, and guiding hearts towards love and truth. RIP
- Stephen Covey – Thank you for your timeless principles of effectiveness and wisdom in leadership and personal growth. RIP
- Dave Chappelle – Thank you for using humor as truth, for speaking boldly in the face of pressure, and your wisdom and wit.
- Sam Sheridan – Thank you for exploring the warriors mind and uncovering the depths of discipline, resilience, and survival.
- John Lovell – Thank you for championing warrior wisdom, preparedness, and living with purpose and conviction.
- Arnold Schwarzenegger – Thank you for proving that vision, discipline, and relentless effort can turn into reality. "Wenn schon, denn schon!"
- Jiddu Krishnamurthi – Thank you for challenging the mind, questioning all authority, and guiding seekers toward self-awareness. RIP
- Omar Suleiman – Thank you for uplifting the ummah.
- Shel Silverstein – Thank you for your whimsical wisdom, boundless imagination, reminding us to find magic in the simplest things, and The Giving Tree. RIP
- Max Ehrmann – Thank you for Desiderata! RIP
- Dr. Joe Dispenza – Thank you for bridging science and spirituality.
- Earl Nightingale – Thank you for illuminating the path to success and the power of thought in shaping destiny. RIP
- Denzel Washington – Thank you for embodying discipline, faith, and purpose. Your wisdom reminds us that success without service is empty, and that true discipline lies in lifting others while staying rooted in principle and humility.
- Jordan Peterson – Thank you for urging us to stand up straight, speak truth with courage, and take responsibility for shaping a meaningful life.

- Whitney Webb – Thank you for your fearless investigative work, exposing hidden truths, and challenging the narratives that shape our world.
- Dr. Gabor Mate – Thank you for your profound insight on healing.
- Shaykh Azhar Sheraze – Thank you for sharing your knowledge, kindness, and compassion.
- Bill Burr – Thank you for reminding me that calling out BS is a spiritual act.
- George Galloway – Thank you for wielding truth like a blade and speaking like a poet at war.
- Thomas Massie – Thank you for being the epitome of an American.
- Ian Carroll – Thank you for reminding us that the pursuit of truth often requires questioning the unquestionable.
- George Carlin – Thank you for preaching sermons disguised as stand-up. RIP
- Agha – Thank you for giving me a strong work ethic and hustle.
- Momma – Thank you for giving me everything, even when you had almost nothing left to give.

I would like to leave you with one last piece of work that I believe that the world should experience.

"Desiderata"

Go placidly amid the noise and haste,
and remember what peace there may be in silence.
As far as possible without surrender
be on good terms with all persons.
Speak your truth quietly and clearly;
and listen to others,
even to the dull and the ignorant;
they too have their story.

Avoid loud and aggressive persons,
they are vexatious to the spirit.
If you compare yourself with others,
you may become vain and bitter;
for always there will be greater and lesser persons than yourself.
Enjoy your achievements as well as your plans.

Keep interested in your own career, however humble;
it is a real possession in the changing fortunes of time.
Exercise caution in your business affairs;
for the world is full of trickery.
But let this not blind you to what virtue there is;
many persons strive for high ideals;
and everywhere life is full of heroism.

Be yourself.
Especially, do not feign affection.
Neither be cynical about love;

for in the face of all aridity and disenchantment
it is as perennial as the grass.

Take kindly the counsel of the years,
gracefully surrendering the things of youth.
Nurture strength of spirit to shield you in sudden misfortune.
But do not distress yourself with dark imaginings.
Many fears are born of fatigue and loneliness.

Beyond a wholesome discipline,
be gentle with yourself.
You are a child of the universe
no less than the trees and the stars;
you have a right to be here.
And whether or not it is clear to you,
no doubt the universe is unfolding as it should.

Therefore be at peace with God,
whatever you conceive Him to be,
and whatever your labors and aspirations,
in the noisy confusion of life keep peace with your soul.

With all its sham, drudgery, and broken dreams,
it is still a beautiful world.
Be cheerful.
Strive to be happy.

–Max Ehrmann

www.ingramcontent.com/pod-product-compliance
Lightning Source LLC
Chambersburg PA
CBHW071747120626
46550CB00002B/698